ROYAL BY BLOOD

JENNIFER JOHNSON

randall house

Royal By Blood

Published by Randall House Publications
114 Bush Road
Nashville, TN 37217

Printed in the United States of America

ISBN 10: 0892655704
ISBN 13: 9780892655700

Dedicated to my three Princess daughters:

Braelyn, Skylar, and Landrey.

You are truly my most beautiful treasures.

TABLE OF CONTENTS

INTRODUCTION

To him who loves us and has freed us from our sins by his blood, and has made us to be a kingdom and priests to serve his God and Father—to him be glory and power for ever and ever! Amen.

Revelation 1:5b, 6

We were created by God to be a part of something larger than ourselves. We were created for something great, something beautiful, and even something royal. In His Word, God says a kingdom is being prepared for us (Matthew 25:34). Throughout Scripture, God calls us children, bride, chosen, blessed, holy, and a royal priesthood. These are a few descriptions of our identity in Christ after we have received His free gift of salvation into our hearts and lives. This salvation is freely bestowed to us through the shedding of Jesus Christ's blood when He died on the cross as the ultimate sacrifice for all. Jesus Christ died to save us from our sins, and He rose again on the third day to give us new life in Him (1 Corinthians 15:3, 4).

For some of you, this news about Jesus' death and resurrection is brand new, and you are curious to know more. For others, these truths have been a part of your head knowledge for many years, but you have yet to understand how it applies to your everyday life. Still for others, you deeply love the One who died and rose again, but you struggle with who you are as a believer. This Bible study will teach each of you who God has created you to be and how to practically live as an heir to His royal kingdom.

In the Bible study *Believing God*, Beth Moore says, "The One who adopted us into His royal family has called us to live according to our legacy." That's exactly what I'm praying *Royal by Blood* will teach us—how to "live according to our legacy." By participating in this Bible study you'll not only know who you are as a member of the royal family, but will learn how a daughter of the King relates to Him, relates to her family, to her friends, and even to herself. I love 1 Timothy 4:12 where Paul tells Timothy "Don't let anyone look down on you because you are young, but set an example for the believers in speech, in love, in life, in faith, and in purity." Through these five areas Paul used to instruct young Timothy, you, too, will explore your royal identity.

Royal by Blood consists of six weeks of lessons divided into five days of study for each week. The first week centers on the subject of your royalty in Christ and our call to be His servant. The remaining five weeks of study is from 1 Timothy 4:12. Each week focuses on one of the five areas in which Paul instructed Timothy to set an example. In each of the five areas, you'll learn how to relate to God, family, friends, and yourself. The daily assignments will guide you to explore God's truths as you read from your Bible and answer relevant questions pertaining to the Scriptures and your life. I also believe this study will cause you to lift your head a little higher because you'll know more intimately to whom you belong.

WEEK 1

ETERNITY IN OUR HEART

Day 1: More to This Life

Today's Scripture:

He has made everything beautiful in its time. He has also set eternity in the hearts of men; yet they cannot fathom what God has done from beginning to end.
Ecclesiastes 3:11

There's an ache, a longing, a hunger in our being that cries out, "There's got to be more to this life." Often we begin to feel this ache when we encounter disappointment . . . from families, friends, circumstances, and the mirror. This disappointment often creates a longing for more—more love, more fun, more joy, more contentment, more beauty, more possessions, or maybe more of something that you can't even define. We just know we want more from what we are already experiencing in life. Something to make us happy. Something to make us content.

When you begin to feel this way about your life, where do these thoughts eventually lead you? To depression? To the mall? To food? To school work? To music?
Write down an action you usually do when the longing for more comes over you.

3   More Love

Sometimes things we do to comfort ourselves become habits in our lives and we don't even know why we do them. We may spend money, eat, exercise, or talk on the phone because deep down inside we have an unmet need we are attempting to satisfy. What is it you long for?

Reread Ecclesiastes 3:11. The phrase "He has set eternity in the hearts of men" speaks about our God-given longing for more than this temporary life on earth. We're created in such a way that we're never satisfied without God—nothing on earth will produce lasting contentment. Define contentment:

Be happy with what you have.

The Amplified Bible says, "He also has planted eternity in men's hearts and minds [a divinely implanted sense of a purpose working through the ages which nothing under the sun but God alone can satisfy.]" I love where it says *sense of purpose* because sometimes we just have that sense or gut feeling that we're on this planet, in our state, in our school, and in our home for more than just going to school and getting a degree. We sense that we do have a unique purpose, but we've yet to discover the details of our destiny.

"We come into this world with a longing to be known and a deep–seated fear that we aren't what we should be."

–John Eldredge, *Sacred Romance*

Same Old Story

Let's look at Jesus' disciples and see what was going on in their young minds. Luke 22:24-30 gives us a glimpse into the disciples' thoughts. In the verses above this passage, we discover that the disciples just finished having the Passover meal, the Last Supper, with Jesus himself. In a complementary account of this story found in John 13:4-7, we also find that Jesus washed their feet as an example of servanthood. This dinner was a great spiritual moment because of the celebration of the Passover with the One who just hours later actually became The Passover Lamb. Now please read Luke 22:24-30.

Old Testament Tip: What's the Passover? Read Exodus chapter 12. When the Israelites were in bondage to Egypt, God called Moses to come before the Pharaoh asking that the Israelites be released. When Pharaoh refused, God sent 10 plagues to change his mind. The final plague—the death of the firstborn—didn't affect the Israelites because they obeyed God's command to put the blood of a lamb on their doorpost. Thus, when God saw the blood, He passed over, sparing them from death. The Israelites then celebrated Passover every year as a remembrance of God's mercy. Second Corinthians 5:7 reveals that Jesus Christ serves as our Passover Lamb. When God sees Christ's presence in our lives, His judgment passes over us!

What do the disciples argue about in Luke 22:24?

Wich one of us is the most important?

It's the same old story! Even the disciples had a deep desire to stand out in a crowd, to make a name for themselves, to be the *greatest*. Read Jesus' response in verses 25-

30. According to verse 26, what two attributes did Jesus tell the disciples they needed if they truly wanted to be great?

the most important is the youngest, and the one who leads is the one has to be like the one who serve

Jesus knows our hearts. He heard the disciples disputing, but more important He saw their longing to *be someone* and to have a title such as "Benefactor." Immediately He tells them, "You are not to be like that." Then in verse 29 He says, "I confer on you a kingdom." Jesus wanted the disciples to stop looking for the world to satisfy their needs, and to look with their spiritual eyes to see the supernatural reality of God's kingdom that belonged to them. Jesus confers, or as the King James Version reads, "appoints" us a kingdom where one day we will eat and drink at His table in His kingdom. There really is more to this life than what we see with our human eyes. "Then the king will say to those on his right, 'Come, you who are blessed by my Father; take your inheritance, the kingdom prepared for you since the creation of the world,'" (Matthew 25:34).

The truths recorded in the Bible are for to us today. His Word is eternal, enduring from generation to generation, no matter how the cultures and ways of the world change. "Jesus Christ is the same yesterday and today and forever," (Hebrews 13:8).

Through *Royal by Blood* we will study the kingdom of God and the amazing privilege we have to be a part of it, as well as the blessed responsibilities that come with being daughters of the King.

Let's pray:

Dear heavenly Father, You are the King of kings and Lord of lords. I bow before You and acknowledge Your divine right to be my authority. My life is not my own. Open my spiritual eyes to see Your kingdom at work in my life, around me, and for others. I want to know in more depth who You are and who You have ordained for me to be. I thank You for what You are going to accomplish in my life because I am obediently studying Your Word. You are good and I love You. In Jesus' name I pray, Amen.

DAY 2: OUR NEW NAME

Today's Scripture:

But you are a chosen people, a royal priesthood, a holy nation, a people belonging to God, that you may declare the praises of him who called you out of darkness into his wonderful light.

1 Peter 2:9

When I was a young girl, I pretended my name was Suzanna, Emily, Kaylyn, or whatever I could think of. I also enjoyed thinking of names for my dolls and stuffed animals. Now I have fun listening to my girls play "next door neighbors" and pretend they have a different name. It's just bred in us, I assume, to think of beautiful names and imagine becoming someone else. When you were younger, what would you pretend?

That I'm a princess named Cinderrolla

Today's lesson is about the beautiful names God gives us the moment we become His by asking His precious Son to forgive our sins and be number one in our lives.

Look up each Scripture and record what Jesus has done for us.

Romans 5:8:

Saved us from ~~the~~ God's anger.

2 Corinthians 5:21:

By CHRIT we are justified

Colossians 2:13:

~~CHRIST gave~~ God gave us life in CHRIST

Old Testament Tip: Before Jesus died on the cross, only appointed priests had the awesome privilege of being in God's presence in what was called the Holy of Holies— the place in the tabernacle/temple where God resided. Once a year the high priest could enter that sacred place to perform the ceremonial duties and meet with God. As Jesus died on the cross, the temple veil was torn in two, signifying that God was inviting all into His glorious presence through His one and only Son, Jesus Christ. (See Matthew 27:50, 51.)

Now look up these verses and record how we are changed after receiving Christ.

2 Corinthians 5:17:

We created again. This is a new life

Romans 8:15, 16:

We are gods children

Ephesians 2:4:

God loves us

No longer are we just "sinners saved by grace," but instead "you also are among those who are called to belong to Jesus Christ . . . and called to be saints," (Romans 1:6, 7). We really become new when we receive God's free gift of salvation and are adopted into the family of God. We are children of God, of the King of all kings. That makes us princesses! We bear His name and are heirs to His kingdom.

Nametags

Notice the Scripture verse for today. Write all the adjectives used to describe believers.

new, children, love, life, saved, gods justified

According to this verse, we're chosen, royal, holy, and belong to God. Compare 1 Peter 2:9 to Exodus 19:5-6. How are the names God called the Old Testament Israelites like those He gives the New Testament believers?

You are a treasor, "Holy Nation people of God".

Believe, dear sister. Whenever you feel a wave of doubt concerning your worth, your value, or your significance, read 1 Peter 2:9 out loud and know that God, our King, sees you as His treasured possession.

Write out Revelation 1:5b,6:

Et que Jésus vous est donné lui le Témoin fidèle, Il est le fils 1er né qui s'est levé au milieu des morts. Il est aussi le chef des Rois de la Terre Jésus Christ nous aime et ils nous a libéré

Let's pray:

Dear glorious heavenly Father, You reign over all. You love me so much that You sent Your only Son to die so I could be free of my sin. Thank You that You raised Jesus from the dead so that I, too, can have new life in You. I pray that I will not only know what You have done for me, but will love You with my whole heart. I bless You today. In Jesus' name I pray, Amen.

de nos péchés par son sang, Il a fait de nous les membres du royaume de Dieu, Il a fait de nous des prêtres pour servir Dieu son père, A Jésus soient la gloire et la puissance pour toujours. Amen.

10

Day 3: In God's Hand

Today's Scripture:

You will be a crown of splendor in the Lord's hand, a royal diadem in the hand of your God.

Isaiah 62:3

Sometimes we can get into a rut of a "woe is me" attitude. Do you find yourself thinking thoughts like: "one day I'll have such and such," "one day I'll be . . ." "one day I'll do . . .," "why me?," or "if only . . . ." So many times we are so busy dreaming of what we wish life was like that we miss what today has to offer. Imagine how different our days could be if we woke up with the attitude of believing "I am blessed." If we believe God is who He says He is and what He says is all truth, then, we are richly blessed in Him.

I know a huge "one day" that most young women spend lots of time dreaming and wondering about—the "one day" their prince will come. They wonder if they have already met their future husband. They idealize about his looks and character. They dream about how they will meet and where they will go for dates. They see themselves being swept away by his love. Yes, I believe in romance and that their desire to one day be married is honorable. But they should not think more about the "one" who is not even a part of their life right now than the One who is.

Match the different names of God to the correct verses.

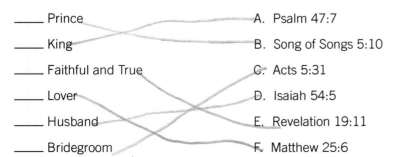

_____ Prince   A. Psalm 47:7

_____ King   B. Song of Songs 5:10

_____ Faithful and True   C. Acts 5:31

_____ Lover   D. Isaiah 54:5

_____ Husband   E. Revelation 19:11

_____ Bridegroom   F. Matthew 25:6

"If God is the Pursuer, the Ageless Romancer, the Lover, then there has to be a beloved, one who is the pursued. This is our role in the story."

-John Eldredge, *The Sacred Romance*

11

God longs to be each of these names to you: Prince, King, Faithful, True, Lover, Husband, and Bridegroom. He wants to show Himself to you in a supernatural way by pursuing you, romancing you. Just think about how He pursues you. When you try to ignore God, He nudges you, uses life experiences to get your attention, brings others to you that reflect His love, plays that song on the radio at just the right moment—what great lengths He goes to! He wants your attention; He wants to call you His own; He wants you to know how much He loves you.

A Father's Love

God also has another name. According to 1 John 3:1, what is this name?

The Father.

As a compassionate father tenderly cares for his own children, your heavenly Father tenderly cares for you. If you have never known this kind of affection from the King, spend some alone time with Him and allow Him the precious opportunity to show His tender side to you.

I remember a difficult season in my young adult years when I was in need of some extra emotional attention. I had my favorite place in my bedroom where I met with my King and it was in those moments that He cuddled me in His love. After I read from His healing Word, I would wrap my arms around my Bible and hug it. I know it sounds silly, but I truly did feel the spiritual sweet embrace of the Lord as I hugged His Word. Listen to this invitation from Deuteronomy 33:12: "'Let the beloved of the LORD rest secure in him, for he shields him all day long, and the one the LORD loves rests between his shoulders.'" That sure sounds like a holy, supernatural hug to me!

What about you, do you have a special place where you meet daily with the Lord? Is there a specific way He has ministered to you?

In my Bed, I don't no.

God our King is all these names to us because He not only loves us, He enjoys us. My family and I like to go to *Chick- fil-A* to eat, and one of my favorite things about the restaurant is what the employees say after you say "thank you." They respond with "It's my pleasure." Isn't that a refreshing response, especially at a fast food restaurant? Let's look at a glimpse of God's motivation for making us His own. Fill in the blanks for each verse.

Ephesians 1:5 "He predestined us to be adopted as his sons through Jesus Christ, in accordance with his ___will___ and ___the good___ ."
___pleasure___

Psalm 18:19 "He brought me out into a spacious place; he rescued me because he ___delighted___ in me."

Isaiah 62:4 "No longer will they call you Deserted, or name your land Desolate. But you will be called ___Ce le qui plait au Seigneur___, and your land ___la bien marree___; for the LORD will take ___pleasure___ in you, and your land will be married."

As God spoke over His people, He still speaks over us, His princesses, today. In Isaiah 62:4, the Hebrew word *Hephzibah* means *my delight is in her.* The word *Beulah* means *married one.* Just as we studied yesterday that we are called by a new name after we become adopted into His royal family by receiving His Son, we see again that our name has changed from *Deserted* or forsaken to the one God takes delight in. Our relationship with God is likened to the intimacy of marriage. When God sent His Son to save us from our sins and rescue us from our own destructed ways, it was not because it was His duty or obligation, but because it gave Him pleasure. When we tell Him "thank You" for all He has done, He really says, "It is my pleasure and always will be."

The last word, *married,* in Isaiah 62:4 means *owned and protected by the Lord.* It's comforting to know that He takes the responsibility upon Himself to protect us, not to allow anyone or anything to snatch us out of His hands (John 10:28).

Let's conclude with the penetrating words of Isaiah 49:16. Write this verse and challenge yourself to memorize it.

Vois j'ai écris ton nom sur la paume de mes mains. Je pense sans arrêt a tes murs de défenses

Let's pray:

Dear heavenly Father, You are my knight in shining armor. You are the One I adore and cherish. Thank you for rescuing me because You delight in me. I humbly come before You today to say that I need to be rescued in the area of _____School_____ *. I delight in being Your princess, Your beloved, Your crown, and royal diadem. Thank You that I am forever Yours. In Jesus' name I pray, Amen.*

Day 4: Our New Clothes

Today's Scripture:

All glorious is the princess within her chamber; her gown is interwoven with gold.

Psalm 45:13

On Day 1 we studied that there is more to life than what we see with our physical eyes. We learned that God has called us into His kingdom. When Jesus spoke about His kingdom, He knew exactly what He was talking about. How? Jesus had been in heaven. That's where Jesus came from before He became man and lived on earth. He knew heaven was real with a real live King on a real throne with real angels surrounding the omnipotent God. In fact, Jesus not only had been there before, but anticipated His own return and our eventual coming. Jesus knew that the Father had put all things under his power, and that he had come from God and was returning to God (John 13:3). Jesus wanted the disciples and us to know that we are a part of this real live kingdom even though we can't see it now with our physical eyes.

What are you to do as we await your departure from this world to your destiny in heaven? You are to prepare yourself; to make yourself ready (Revelation 19:7). Your Groom is patiently awaiting your "walk down the aisle" so the two of you can live happily ever after. Look up and write out Hosea 2:19:

J'enlèverai de sa bouche le nom des Baals, et personne ne se souviendra plus d'eux

Read the parable of the Wedding Banquet in Matthew 22:1-14. This story mentions wedding clothes. Reread Matthew 22:12 and write the question asked the arriving man.

Friend How did you come in here without a wedding garment

It was customary for the host to provide wedding clothes for individuals invited to the wedding banquet. In the above parable, the man did not accept the free gift of the wedding clothes. What happened to this man according to verse 13?

15

They bind his hand and foot and put him outside in the darkness

Then he will weeping and gnashing of teeth

Ladies, please don't just read about the good news of the kingdom of God, answer Jesus' invitation with a definite "yes!" Being prepared for His coming simply begins with a "yes."

A Heavenly Wardrobe

Deep down inside all of us females, whether we play in the dirt or have our nails done every week, we long for complete acceptance and . . . a fabulous wardrobe.

Read the verses below that describe the clothes prepared for the bride of Christ: "Hallelujah! For our Lord God Almighty reigns. Let us rejoice and be glad and give him glory! For the wedding of the Lamb has come, and his bride has made herself ready. Fine linen, bright and clean was given to her to wear," (Revelation 19:6b-8).

In the Old Testament the priests had to physically wear specific garments made by those whom the Holy Spirit skilled. The garments were made of beautiful blue, purple and scarlet yarn, and white linen with real gold and jewels positioned in specified places. One of the purposes of these garments is mentioned in Exodus 28:2: "And thou shalt make holy garments for Aaron thy brother for glory and for beauty" (KJV). The NIV translates the word *glory* as *dignity* and the word *beauty* as *honor*.

Remember from 1 Peter 2:9 that we are part of the royal priesthood? The clothes we literally wear in the supernatural, seen with spiritual eyes, are also for our glory, dignity, beauty, and honor. My favorite article of clothing worn by Old Testament priests was a pure gold plate attached to the turban worn over the forehead. Look up Exodus 28:36 and write what was engraved on this plate of pure gold.

un bijou d'or pure en forme de fleur. Gravé "consacré au Seigneur".

Princess, if there was ever something to write on your mirror to see every morning it's these magnificent words—HOLY TO THE LORD. How differently would you see yourself if you wholeheartedly believed you were holy to the Lord, meaning your mind, body, spirit and soul were all good?

Turn in your Bible to Isaiah 61:10 and fill in the blanks.
"I delight greatly in the LORD; my soul rejoices in my God. For he has ___Saved___ me with garments of ___Salut___ and arrayed me in a ___clothe___ of righteousness, as a bridegroom adorns his head like a priest, and as a bride adorns herself with her ___Bijou___ ."

As Jonah 2:9 says, "Salvation comes from the LORD." We spiritually wear our salvation that we totally, 100% received from God. Having salvation on means we are no longer our own, but now we belong to the One who purchased us through His death and resurrection. It also means we are eternal beings—our spirit will not see death, but will live forever with God in heaven. Because we spiritually wear a robe of righteousness means that God no longer sees us in our messiness, our sin, but sees us as having right standing before Him. With salvation comes forgiveness, with forgiveness comes purity. He washes the sin, the ugliness off of us and leaves us sparkling clean. Standing before Him now wearing these royal garments "The King is enthralled by your beauty; honor him for he is your Lord," (Psalm 45:11).

Let's pray:
Dear heavenly Father, I stand before You now dressed as Your bride adorned in Your salvation and in Your righteousness. Thank you that when You look at me You see beauty. Help me to see myself through Your eyes. I love and praise You, my King. In Jesus' precious name I pray, Amen.

Day 5: Royalty Serves

Today's Scripture:

But because my servant, Caleb, has a different spirit and follows me wholeheartedly.
Numbers 14:24

Old Testament Tip: When the Israelites were delivered from Egyptian bondage, God promised them a land "flowing with milk and honey." God led them to this land and told the Israelites to capture it. The Israelites then sent 12 spies to survey the land and its inhabitants. Caleb was one of the 12 spies sent into the Promised Land. When the spies returned, all except Joshua and Caleb voted not to attack the people because they appeared too strong. With that decision God pronounced judgment on that generation of Israelites for their unbelief. He foretold that all of them would wander in the wilderness and die there, never entering the Promised Land . . . all, that is, except for Joshua and Caleb. God rewarded Caleb for following Him completely and believing that God meant what He said. That's the story behind our key verse today. To read the full story and get all the details, check out Numbers 14.

Throughout the past four days, we have studied how God pursues us with an invitation to be a part of His kingdom. We found out that after accepting His invitation, we are now royalty, a princess in His eyes. On Day 3 we discovered some amazing names of God and how He is intimate with us. Yesterday we examined our spiritual clothes—the righteous covering God places over us.

For the next 5 weeks we will be focusing on our responsibilities as princesses. Through the instruction Paul gave to Timothy in 1 Timothy 4:12, we will study how to "set an example for the believer in speech, in life, in love, in faith, and in purity."

18

Before we get to the heart of today's lesson, I want to show you in Scripture one more "very necessary" accessory. Look up each verse and write the name of the accessory all princesses must have:

Psalm 21:3: _happyness benedictions, a gold crown_

Revelation 4:4: _gold crown, white clothes_

Isaiah 61:3: _un turban, huile perfuming, party clothes_

Fact, Not Fiction

Yes, Princess, this is no fairy-tale. I am convinced that in the spiritual realm, we are wearing a most beautiful crown of gold on our heads (2 Timothy 4:8). I even think that all of God's heavenly host of angels and the spirits of darkness can see it and identify us as belonging to the King. We don't need to seek an earthly "crown" because we already have one.

Now that we know we are royalty, let's look at our responsibility. Look up the following verses and fill in the blanks.
Revelation 5:10 "You have made them to be a _King_ and _priest_ to _priest_ our God, and they will reign on the earth."

Hebrews 9:14 "How much more, then, will the blood of Christ, who through eternal Spirit offered himself unblemished to God, cleanse our conscience from acts that lead to death, so that we may _serve_ the living God."

Luke 1:38 "'I am the Lord's _maid servant_,' Mary answered. 'May it be to me as you have said.' Then the angel left her."

Matthew 20:28 "Just as the Son of Man did not come to be a ___Served___ , but to ___Serve___ , and to give his life as a ransom for many."

As daughters of the King, we are called to serve our King with our lives. If you have grown up in church or been in church for several years, no doubt, you have heard plenty of sermons on servanthood. You've heard messages encouraging you to know your spiritual gift, and use it as your service to Him and to the church. I pray that you already have a place of service in the church or community. If you do serve your church or community, in what way(s) do you help others? Is it in the nursery, the youth ministry, or maybe in a food kitchen?

In the nursery.

> "God determines your greatness by how many people you serve, not how many people serve you."
>
> –Rick Warren, *The Purpose Driven Life*

What I want you to know first is who you are in Christ. Then you can serve Christ out of a heart of gratitude and humility, remembering all He has done for you. To have your significance and security in Christ enables you to lay aside your own needs and agendas to bless someone else.

To be a servant of Jesus means we are devoted to His will. As servants we bind ourselves to Him in such closeness that our desires become His. I have found the most joy in my personal life when I consider others as more important than myself (Philippians 2:4). Has there been a time when you did something for someone else when you got nothing in return? How did that make you feel?

We bought food for the homeless people (Hungry people) they took it but nothing sometimes for others things make me feel like they are not happy But I knew that what I did was good

20

Look at the Scripture verse for today. Fill in the blank with *your* name. "But because my servant, _Emma_ , has a different spirit and follows me wholeheartedly."

Let's pray:

Dear heavenly Father, You are my master, my Lord. As Mary and as Caleb thought differently from the way the world thinks, so I, too, want to think like a daughter of Yours and as a servant. I desire to follow You completely even when it is difficult or when I just do not want to. Thank You for sending Your Son, Jesus, to be an example of servanthood for me. I want to be like Him. In Jesus' name I pray, Amen.

WEEK 2

GRACIOUS SPEECH

DAY 1: BEAUTIFUL LIPS

Today's Scripture:

He who loves a pure heart and whose speech is gracious will have the king for his friend.

Proverbs 22:11

Our focus this week and the next four weeks is based on the instruction Paul gave Timothy. In 1 Timothy 4:12 Paul told Timothy, "Don't let anyone look down on you because you are young, but set an example for the believers in speech, in life, in love, in faith, and in purity." We will study in detail each one of these areas (speech, life, love, faith, and purity) as they relate to our relationship with God, with others, and ourselves. As a princess of the King, even in your youth, you are to set a godly example to those around you through your daily life. My hope is that through this study of God's Word, you will learn how to think, act, and be blessed by living the privileged life of a princess.

We ended Week 1's study with the principle of servanthood. I hope you are already beginning to see that belonging to God's royal family is not only a privilege, but also a responsibility. I am privileged to be under the care and providence of my Shepherd Lord Jesus, and yet I also understand my responsibility to listen to His voice as He daily directs me. In the children's book *A Parable About The King* by Beth Moore, the king explains to his princess daughter, "you will never be happy until you accept both the privilege and responsibility that goes with belonging to me." I am completely convinced that lasting happiness is found in knowing whose we are and what our purpose is. In today's study let's learn how servanthood is connected to our speech.

Fill in the blanks for Colossians 3:17: "And __whatever__ you do, whether in __word__ or __deed__ , do it __all__ in the name of the Lord Jesus, giving thanks to God the Father through him."

This is a very startling verse! Paul reminds us that everything we say or do needs to have the stamp of Jesus on it. Sometimes this is easy and sometimes not so easy. For instance, when I am at church I tend to say things that are pleasing to God. But sometimes when I am irritated with my children, I tend to say things I eventually regret.

When is it easier for you to say things pleasing to God?

At church, or when i'm happy...

When is it not so easy to have pleasing words?

When I am furious, or am irrated...

In your answers, did you state that your hardest times are with family? No doubt, it is hard to serve the Lord through our words with those we live with everyday. Perhaps the biggest challenge is to serve our siblings with our speech! I'm sure you can name a dozen different things your parents or caregivers told you over and over regarding what you are to say or not to say toward a brother or sister! Name some of those directives:

Clean your room, don't speak when you are eating, don't play computer a long time...

Gracious Lips

The title for this week's study comes from an interesting verse in Proverbs. In fact, it's the Scripture verse for today. Please review the verse. The King James Version of Proverbs 22:11 says, "He that loveth pureness of heart, for the grace of his lips the king shall be his friend." I love that expression "for the grace of his lips." (Too bad we can't purchase a lipstick called "for the grace of your lips" that would guarantee pleasant words as we wore it!) The word *grace* in the Hebrew language (the original language of the Old Testament) means "graciousness, kindness, favor, or objective beauty: favor, grace, pleasant, precious, well-favored." This word *grace* comes from the word that means "to bend or stoop in kindness to an inferior." Let this sink in for a moment. "To bend or stoop in kindness to an inferior." Could this mean toward a younger brother or sister who continually annoys every fiber of your being? Or an older sibling who constantly belittles or ignores? Ouch! These must be the hardest persons in the world to serve with grace in our speech. And yet, they are not an exception to those whom God has called us to show kindness to through our words.

Look up the following Scriptures and explain (in your own words) what God is telling us as a princess.

Matthew 5:43-47:

We shall not hate our ennemi, we shall love our neighboor and our ennemi

Luke 6:27-36:

We have to folow Jesus and let evrythings beaind us.

Unfortunately, those in our own homes may seem more like enemies than family sometimes. But God instructs us to speak words of blessing toward them. Trust me, I know the last thing you feel like doing is praying a blessing over those who mistreat you. Did you know you will never look more like your King as when you choose gracious words over angry words? Instead of ugly insults and remarks lashed back at those hurling hurtful words at you, you can grace them with your kind lips. Ecclesiastes 10:12 says, "Words from a wise man's mouth are gracious, but a fool is consumed by his own lips." God is calling us as daughters, sisters, and friends to be wise with our mouths even toward those we think do not deserve it.

Let Jesus be our example and cause others to wonder where our words of grace come from. Look up and write Luke 4:22.

Tout le monde s'étonne est dans l'admiration et s'étonne des pardes merveilleuses qui sortent de la bouch ils disent: "Pourt gui cette Homme la c'est bien le fils de Joseph

Let's pray:

Dear heavenly Father, Because of Your beautiful grace extended to me, I choose to extend grace to ___Jack___ . Forgive me, Father, for any hurtful words I have said. I pray that you will show me a specific way I can serve my brother or sister with my words. I pray that I will know how to pray for my brother or sister. Thank you, Jesus, for the gift of grace. I love you. In Jesus' name I pray. Amen.

DAY 2: DEMONSTRATION OF THE SPIRIT

Today's Scripture:

My message and my preaching were not with wise and persuasive words, but with a demonstration of the Spirit's power.

1 Corinthians 2:4

My husband, Richard, came to believe in the Lord Jesus and confessed before men that Jesus is Lord when he was a freshman in college. Richard did not grow up in a family who attended church, but when a friend on campus invited him to a local church he was eager to go. Richard was interested in going to church because he had been hanging out with this friend and four other guys at the Baptist Student Union (now called Baptist Collegiate Ministry) where they spent much of their time between classes and enjoyed one another's friendship. He admits that the real reason he first went to the BSU was because of the free ping pong and the girls he met. But it was through the authentic lives of these five believing guys who readily talked about their personal relationship with the Lord that encouraged Richard to receive salvation from the Lord. During a fall revival at the local church, Richard felt the conviction of the Lord to go forward and pray with the pastor to become a believer, a new person in the Lord, a saint, and a prince. All five of these guys were in our wedding and just moments before the ceremony they gathered around Richard and prayed blessings upon his new life as a husband. These men were powerful witnesses of the Lord in my husband's life.

Yesterday, we looked at being a servant through our speech especially with family members. Today let's look at servanthood with our words towards those who are not Christians (which may very well still be your family).

Have you ever tried to witness to someone about your faith in God?

You yes to a friend

If so, what was your motivation?

To do what Jesus tells me to do and to have som oere that canspeak about God at school

If not, what are your fears?

Most of us have plenty of reasons why we don't share our faith with an unbeliever. It doesn't seem to come naturally to us. Some of you, though, may have had lots of practice, and it's getting easier to share your faith in God. After completing today's lesson, I hope sharing your faith will become even easier for all of us whether we are comfortable witnessing or have never tried.

What is Paul's main point to the Romans about the non-believers in Romans 10:14,15?

Il faut que quelqu'un dnncn pour savoir...

28

Il faut croire pour lui parler
Il faut en tendre parler de lui pour croire
Il faut quelqu'un d'envoyer pour cela
pour annoncer

What responsibility did Jesus give believers in Matthew 28:19,20?

Go to all the people in the world and Baptize them, Teach them to Obey my commandment And I will be with you forever and ever

In 2 Corinthians 5:20, what name does Paul use to describe Christians?

Just

One fear many identify as a reason not to speak up about Christ is being scared of not knowing what to say or lacking the "guts" to speak up. How does God answer that? From the following verses write the phrase surrounding the word *power*.

Acts 1:8: *Mais vous allez recevoir une force celle de l'esprit saint qui descendra sur vous*

Acts 4:33: *Avec une grande force les apôtres témoignent que jésus s'est relevé de la mort*

Ephesians 1:19: *la puissance extraordinaire que Dieu a montré pour nous*

1 Thessalonians 1:5: *Avec la puissance et l'aide du Saint esprit*

2 Timothy 1:7: *et esprit rempli de force*

According to the first verse, Acts 1:8, where does the power God gives us come from?

It comes from the Holy spirit

This power comes from the Holy Spirit who lives within us (1 Corinthians 6:19). The Holy Spirit takes up residency within us the moment we accept Jesus as our Savior (Ephesians 1:13,14).

When Jesus left this earth to go back to the Father in heaven, what did He promise the disciples (and us!)? Check out John 14:15-17.

He promises to give us the Holy Spirit, someone who will help us and be with us forever...

Paul tells us in Ephesians 1:20 that the power of the Holy Spirit is just like the power God used to raise Jesus from the dead. WOW! This word *power* comes from the Greek word *dunamis*. It's where we get our word *dynamite*. *Dunamis* means miraculous power. Witnessing to someone may not seem natural because it isn't natural; it is SUPERnatural. The power God gave to each believer is not our own; it's God's miraculous power flowing from our mouths into the listener's hearts.

When God prompts you to share with an individual or group about Him, you can simply pray that the Holy Spirit will demonstrate God's power through your words and actions, then leave the results in God's hands.

Philip's Story

Let's conclude today's study with an interesting and amazing story. Please read Acts 8:26-35 and answer the following questions.

Who prompted Philip to talk to the Ethiopian (verse 29)?

the Holy Spirit

Did Philip hesitate after the prompting (verse 30)?

No !

What was the Ethiopian's response to Philip's question (verse 31)?

How? Nobody explain me.

According to verse 34 do you think the Ethiopian wanted to understand?

Yes I'm sure

God knows what He is doing. We are so privileged to be able to join Him. God wonderfully allowed Philip the blessed opportunity to be a part of the Ethiopian's salvation experience. When God prompts us to speak to someone about Him, the Holy Spirit is most likely already at work.

At the end of this story it says that "the Spirit of the Lord suddenly took Philip away." This was a literal disappearance to another location where Philip continued to preach the gospel of Jesus Christ. I have never heard of God doing that to anyone in today's time, but I do know personally that after I have obeyed God through blessing someone with my words, I feel like I have been lifted to "cloud 9." I remember one time when the Lord told me to share a particular personal testimony with a large group of women. I was very nervous about speaking in front of these women because I barely knew them. I chose to obey by testifying what I felt led to say. After the event, as soon as I got in my car, I heard God whisper to my heart "thank you." I simply said "You're welcome," and was awed that my God, who is the God of the universe, would thank *me*. I believe God is looking for those He can demonstrate His power through. He desires to speak even through *you*. May you desire your words to glorify God and show off the miraculous power of the Holy Spirit today and every day.

Let's pray:

Dear heavenly Father, Thank you for the gift of the Holy Spirit. I pray that I will be sensitive to Your promptings, and that I will be bold to proclaim the good news of Jesus Christ. Thank you that You will demonstrate Your power through me by the Holy Spirit. I give You all the glory! In Jesus' name I pray, Amen.

Day 3: So That We Can

Today's Scripture:

Who comforts us in all our troubles so that we can comfort those in any trouble with the comfort we ourselves have received from God.

2 Corinthians 1:4

Princess, I hope you are having a good day. I hope that you are keeping your head high knowing you belong to the King of all kings. You dwell in the shelter of the Most High (Psalm 91:1). You're His "treasured possession" (Exodus 19:5). What is important to you today is important to your Dad, the King.

What is on your mind today (on this day _09_ / _12_ / _12_)?

School, that we have to trust in God and God will help us

Unless you share with someone, no one else can know what you wrote or how you're feeling. No one, that is, except God. God can. He sees.

A woman in the Bible named Hagar ran away from home because she had been mistreated. The angel of the Lord came to her and spoke blessings of comfort and instruction over her. Then, "she gave this name to the LORD who spoke to her: 'You are the God who sees me,'" (Genesis 16:13).

Say that phrase back to the Lord out loud: "You are the God who sees me."

Just as Hagar was found by the Lord near a spring in the desert (Genesis 16:7), where in specifics geographically does God find you today?

2, le bois fleuri 27750 la couture Boussey France.

Dans la campagne

Where does God find you emotionally?

tired, and stressed, scary, a little but happy

We can assume that Hagar was scared, lonely, angry, confused, and troubled with her present circumstances. God saw her, but what else did the angel say, "the _____ has _____ of your _____." I believe that through this angelic visit, Hagar was comforted. Hagar now knew with her heart and mind that God cared for her, understood her trouble, and had answers for her confusion. God told Hagar to go back home, and gave her specific instructions concerning the son in her womb.

Describe a time when you knew without a shadow of doubt that God heard you.

For a test I prayed and God heard me because I wrote me concentrer et me rappeler J'ai bien pu ...

How can specific instructions given directly to us and our circumstances be comforting?

We have to obey God

I do find comfort in instructions for my life because it gives me a peace that I am where I am supposed to be and doing what God wants me to do. The peace in my life eliminates confusion and inner turmoil.

Are you being careful to obey the instructions given to you either by God or someone in authority? Do you understand that by obeying you will gain comfort with some peace of mind?

Yes, because it's strongs personsi... Yes, because we obey

Me and God

I'm sure you have been thinking, *how does all this relate to the topic of speech*? Good question.

Alone time with God, hearing from God, is necessary so that we can be readily available to be a witness through our speech. Fill in the blanks of 2 Corinthians 1:4. "Who comforts us in all our _tribulation_ so that we can comfort those in _trouble_ _____ with the comfort we ourselves have received from God."

Look again at 2 Corinthians 1:4. The first and third *comfort* comes from the same Greek word *parakiesis*. The second *comfort* comes from a different Greek word *parakaleo*. The first and third *comfort* refers to the consolation and exhortation we receive from God Himself. The second *comfort* refers to an invitation to be comforted. In our English language it is hard sometimes to get the whole meaning of certain Scriptures without the help of looking at the original language. We can learn that we are not called to do all the comforting toward someone; instead we are to comfort them by pointing them to the best Comforter of all—the One who comforted us—Jesus Christ. "For the LORD comforts his people and will have compassion on his afflicted ones," (Isaiah 49:13).

Be in a place—emotionally and spiritually—where God can minister to you. Ask Him to do the impossible in your circumstances. Ask Him to fill your heart completely and to help you love Him with an undivided heart. Pour your heart out before Him and allow Him to fill you with His love.

Receive His forgiveness for your sins. Receive His unfailing love for your hurts. Receive His joy for your sorrows. Receive His heart for your hardened heart. Receive His Spirit for your desires. Receive His grace for your unworthiness. Receive His mercy for your failures. Receive His favor for your dreams. Receive His sufficiency for your unmet needs. Receive His humility for your self-righteousness.

God wants to use you to be a witness to those around you. Do not wait for someone "more qualified" to come along and do the work. When you allow yourself to be ministered to by God through the Word of God, you are available for God to shine through you. You can do it!

Pray for an opportunity for God to allow you to comfort someone else. Then in the space below record the way God spoke to you about the person and how God spoke through you.

"Praise be to the God and Father of our Lord Jesus Christ, the Father of compassion and the God of all comfort," (2 Corinthians 1:3).

Let's pray:
Dear heavenly Father, Thank You for Your comfort that comforts me in all my troubles. I pray that I, too, can comfort someone else by showing them You. In Jesus' name I pray, Amen.

Day 4: To the Lord

Today's Scripture:

Speak to one another with psalms, hymns, and spiritual songs. Sing and make music in your heart to the Lord.

Ephesians 5:19

Is there a more appropriate response to the comfort and help we receive from "the One who sees me" than to use our mouths to praise and thank God? We're living in such an exciting and blessed time where worship music is so prevalent, fun, and powerful. This generation has the most artists, styles, concerts, and technological equipment to enjoy music than ever before. I believe this rise of anointed Christian artists is a gift from the Lord to His children. God is pouring out His Spirit on willing servants who are humbly using their talents to lift up the name of the Lord through song. And it is beautiful! What are some of your favorite Christian songs?

"Bless it be the name of the Lord..."
"Prince of peace",

Why do you like these songs . . . What is it about the songs that speak to you?

the scriptures, and just the music

I listen to music and sing for several reasons depending on my mood or circumstances. I may sing because I need encouragement to keep my focus on God, or because it takes away feelings of loneliness, or simply because I like the song. Another reason

I choose to sing is in direct response to answered prayer. Those are times I sing the loudest and from the inner depths of my soul.

Let's look at some of God's people who had a joyous song to sing to their Lord.
Look up the following Scriptures and record the event and write the names of the ones who sang.

Exodus 14:29-15:1:

Moses and the Israelites

Ezra 3:10-13:

All, the peoples, les levites, les prêtres...

Luke 1:39-55:

Mary, Elisabeth

In each of these recorded events God's people broke out in spontaneous praise and thanksgiving through song. God had delivered His people from their enemies, allowed the Israelites to begin rebuilding the temple, and confirmed the truth of the angel's news to Mary. In the Exodus and Ezra passages God's people experienced a corporate time of worship; they worshiped together as families for a common purpose.

Can you think of a time you experienced a corporate gathering of believer's spontaneous response to God that resulted in worship through song? Describe the circumstances and the way it made you feel.

Yes, in a church. She sang a song alone when nobody was singing I was surprised But joyful too.

38

In the Luke passage we see that God can do something just for us personally that cannot be explained any other way but Him. Mary had her own song to sing. Can you think of a time God ministered personally to you that caused you to rejoice through song? Describe your time with the Lord.

When he did something incredible
for me, I want to sing a shout
and ...

Old Testament Tip: Have you ever heard of the book of Psalms found in the middle of the Bible? Um . . . did you know that it is entirely made up of SONGS? Yep, *psalm* means *song*. The book of Psalms (or songs) is the hymnal or songbook of the Israelites. Christians have incorporated portions of these songs into their lyrics throughout the history of Christianity. Challenge yourself to learn some new songs by reading through Psalms. And if you're feeling particularly musical, create new melodies and music to share with others . . . or to use in your personal worship.

I'm a big believer in worshiping together with a church family and in having our own private worship at home. I believe both contribute to healthy growth in our relationship with our King. I know that the word "worship" conjures up a lot of different images and meanings, but as I relate to you today, I am referring to the actual worship through song. In the book *The Prayer That Changes Everything,* Stormie O'Martian writes, "One of the most important things you can do in your life is to worship together with other believers. I can't emphasize that enough. This kind of *corporate* praise can pull you in and take you someplace you couldn't get without it. There is something that happens when we worship God together with other believers that does not happen to the same degree when we don't. There's a renewing, reviving, and refreshing of our own souls. It is amazingly life-transforming, and when you let yourself be swept up into it, it will melt and change your heart. But if you have to always rely on a group to draw you in, you are missing an important element in your personal walk with God. Your own spirit and soul need to connect with God in a way that can only happen through frequent and ongoing praise and worship."

Do you agree with Stormie OMartian? If so, in what way?

Yes, I think it's very important to praise and worship god everyday

"Sing praises to God, sing praises; sing praises to our King, sing praises" (Psalm 47:6).

For our time of prayer today, take a moment to sing a song to your King. I promise it will be beautiful to Him no matter how you sound!

Day 5: Those Who Listen

Today's Scripture:

Do not let any unwholesome talk come out of your mouths, but only what is helpful for building others up according to their needs, that it may benefit those who listen.
Ephesians 4:29

As you think back on this week's study, was there something in particular that stood out for you as new truth or that sincerely ministered to you?

All of those study's. The comfort of god

I want to answer that question, too. I loved the discovery of the two different Greek words for the word *comfort* in Day 3. Understanding the difference revolutionized my courage and confidence in reaching out to someone in need. The pressure is off of me because during those times of not knowing how to help someone, I now feel that I can do something—I can tell them about the comfort God has given me and invite them to find lasting comfort by seeking God.

Be prepared—today's study will probably "get into your business." How can we discuss the topic of speech without addressing one of the biggest problems we as women have—gossiping. I was participating with our youth group during a Wednesday night service and the youth minister (who also happens to be my husband) asked the group, "What makes you angry?" A sophomore girl immediately responded with "gossip." What I think is so crazy is that all of us as women hate gossip, and yet it's also one of the most difficult temptations to avoid. We need help, right? We need divine help!

In your own words what is the definition of gossip?

Laugh about peoples badly a be
mean with what we say about the
others.

What motivates people to gossip?

The others is different, when someone

What motivates you to gossip?

The persons at school, when someon
is wird or different

41

Sticks and Stones

Have you ever heard the saying, "Sticks and stones may break my bones, but words will never hurt me"? It's true that it would hurt if someone hurled sticks and stones at us, but it also hurts when people say mean, false, and hurtful things to us. Why do we hate gossip? Because it hurts! You may have been a victim of gossip or you may have seen someone you love hurt by gossip. My prayer is that Satan will not get any more mileage from this offense, but that God would truly heal as you believe God's truth over your particular situation.

Proverbs 26:2 says, "Like a fluttering sparrow or a darting swallow, an undeserved curse does not come to rest." Princess, if the rumor told about you is not true, then it will not be a part of your identity. Whatever was said will not come to rest on you or your name. Understanding the truth that the "curse" will not identify you will set you free from shame, condemnation, fear of others, fear of not having favor with others, and of wanting to hide. I believe you're free to keep your head held high knowing you are not the "curse." What does God want to do with the curse? Write out Deuteronomy 23:5.

Mais le seigneur votre, Dieu n'a pas voulu
écouter Balaam. Il a changé pour
vous la malédiction en bénédiction
par ce qu'il vous aime

King David also understood the hurt caused by someone saying something that was not true. He prayed in 2 Samuel 16:12 that "the LORD will see my distress and repay me with good for the cursing I am receiving today." David even had rocks and dirt thrown at him as he was walking. But, verse 13 says that David continued to his destination. Princess, do not let whatever was said of you stop you from doing what God has planned for you. If you're scared to go to class, GO. If you're scared to go back to church, GO. If you're scared to try out for a position, GO. If you're scared to go back to work, GO. If you're scared to go back home, GO. "But you will not leave in haste or go in flight; for the LORD will go before you, the God of Israel will be your rear guard," (Isaiah 52:12). Be wise in your going and know that your King is protecting you. What do we do with the curse? First Peter 2:21-23 can answer this question. From Jesus' example what can we learn to do with gossip said either directly or indirectly about us?

don't answer and ~~be~~ trust in God with. I ignore it

That's right. We are going to have to choose to ignore it. We also are going to have to "entrust" ourselves "to him who judges justly." We have to trust God that He will take care of us and the situation and the one speaking the gossip.

Ready, Aim, Fire

Just as you have been hurt by gossip whether directly or indirectly, you may have also hurt others. Read James 3:5-10. To what does James compare the damage of a bad "tongue" (hurtful speech)?

flamme can put fire in a forest

How can a fire damage?

détruire

How does poison damage?

tuer

How can gossip damage?

faire du mal

The Scripture verse for today is Ephesians 4:29. The Amplified Bible which translates a few words directly from the original Greek language says, "Let no foul *or* polluting language, *nor* evil word *nor* unwholesome *or* worthless talk [ever] come out of your mouth, but only such [speech] as is good *and* beneficial to the spiritual progress of

43

others, as is fitting to the need *and* the occasion, that it may be a blessing *and* give grace (God's favor) to those who hear it."

In the space below, list words or phrases that you have said today that could be defined as unwholesome or helpful talk.

Unwholesome   **Helpful**

- C'est bon! Arrête!   - I will help you
- Tu m'énerve   mum
- (Screaming)   - Je t'aime
- Dépeche toi!   - Ça va
                                                    aller
- J'en ai marre!   - C'est pas
- Ça se fait pas!   grave

Something that I hear time and time again from my own children is, "But she made me say it." No one can make us say anything. They may cause us to want to say something, but we are ultimately, completely responsible for the words out of our mouths. Ephesians 4:29 says, "Do not let . . . " We can stop ourselves from saying something unwholesome and hurtful. We just need to be more cautious, conscious, and responsible about the words we use.

Proverbs 18:8 and Proverbs 26:22 say exactly the same thing: "The words of a gossip are like choice morsels; they go down to a man's inmost parts."

For those who are listening to us, let us be the one to encourage, build up, inspire, and give hope. According to Proverbs 12:14, 13:2, and 18:20, how will God reward those who speak kindness?

Donner un salaire, tirer profit de ses paroles; manger grâce à ses paroles, l'aider à gagner sa vie

To end this study, write out Galatians 5:14-15.

(14) Toute la loi de moïse est contenu dans un seul commandement! "tu dois aimer ton prochain comme toi même. (15) mais si vous vous mordez et si vous vous blessez les uns les autres, attention, vous allez vous détruire!"

Let's pray:

Dear heavenly Father, I pray that You will shut the mouths of those cursing me. I also pray that You will put a guard over my mouth so I will only speak helpful words to those who are listening to me. In Jesus' name I pray, Amen.

WEEK 3

LIVING LIFE WITH A RIGHT PERSPECTIVE

DAY 1: OUR CITIZENSHIP

Today's Scripture:

But our citizenship is in heaven. And we eagerly await a Savior from there, the Lord Jesus Christ.

Philippians 3:20

One of my family's favorite topics to discuss is heaven. Our daughters take turns saying what they know about heaven. Then they ask plenty of questions, which my husband and I try to answer. Questions like, "I wonder what is on the feast table tonight in heaven?" As we talk about it, I always remind them that our *real* home is in heaven. One day my youngest daughter completely grasped this fact. I knew she had received the truth because she seriously asked, "Mommy, if this isn't our real home, then why did you paint the walls?" What could I say except that God made the colors, and this is only a taste of the strikingly gorgeous colors we will behold in heaven!

In the space below, list everything you know about heaven. (Isn't it exciting and comforting to know that a place of celebration awaits us!)

Dieu est assis sur un trone, on va chanter et danser tous ensemble, les anges, la table ou nous mangerons tous l'agneau

In Week 1 you studied the kingdom of God. You've already written down thoughts about heaven. Now, I want you to list what the word *kingdom* represents.

Ensemble de personnes et des maisons avec un roi et un palais.

Good. I'm sure you would agree with me that the kingdom of God incorporates the domain of God, His rule as King, His realm, and His sovereignty. Heaven is a part of His kingdom. Heaven is the name of His eternal domain. God's kingdom, though, is wherever His presence is. For instance, according to the Lord's Prayer in Matthew 6:10 what are we instructed to pray?

Que Son regne et royaume vienne et que Sa volonté se réalise.

God allows us the amazing privilege to pray that as His will is accomplished in heaven, may it also be accomplished on earth, our realm of existence.

Three insightful verses in Matthew offer a glimpse into how God may answer that portion of the Lord's Prayer. Look up the following verses and write what was preached and the action following.

48

Matthew 4:23:

Jesus prechait la bonne nouvelle, dans
les maisons et guerrissait les malades
et les douleurs.

Matthew 9:35:

Jésus prèche la Bonne Nouvelle et enseigne
dans les maisons juives guerissait les
maladies et les douleurs-

Matthew 10:7:

"Le royaume de Dieu est tout
près de vous"

Jesus and the disciples preached the good news of the kingdom and then showed
people what it looked like. The good news preached is the simple gospel of Jesus who
died and rose again so we can have a relationship with God and enter into the eternal
home He has prepared for us. After people heard the good news of the kingdom, many
gloriously, supernaturally experienced it. Hallelujah! I believe Jesus wants us to know
and experience this real kingdom. It's not a fairytale. It's truth.

The Real Thing

It seems that many people try to create their own kingdoms. Perhaps the truth from
Ecclesiastes 3:11, "He has set eternity in the hearts of men," (Week 1, Day 1) applies
to this. God has set eternity in our hearts, being a part of His kingdom is where we
belong. But those who reject God try to fill that void with something else. Our culture
glamorizes people who have a lot of material possessions, fame, "people" to do this
and that, etc. How many televisions shows revolve around the luxury of mansions,
multiple vehicles, elaborate wardrobes and jewelry, numerous staff, buildings and
property, and unlimited financial resources? Seem like they are trying to build a

kingdom to me. But what does the future for these folks look like? Psalm 49:10-20 offers us a description of the destiny of unbelieving wealthy. Summarize what it says.

Ils vont habiter dans la tombe pour toujours, et la mort sera leur berger. Il ne verra plus jamais la lumière, Ils mourront comme les animaux, Ils von perdre leurs richesses

What is our future? God has purposed an earthly destiny and an eternal destiny for all of us. For those who have received God's free gift of salvation, our eternal destiny is our heavenly real home where we already have citizenship. Reread the Scripture verse for today. That's good news, princess!

Without our eternal destiny as believers, we have no worthwhile earthly destiny. They fit together perfectly. Write out 2 Corinthians 4:18.

Nous ne cherchons pas ce qu'on peut voir, nous cherchons les choses qu'on ne voit pas. En effet ce qu'on peut voir ne dure pas longtemps. Mais les choses qu'on voit durent toujours.

Our physical eyes and the eyes of our heart are to be looking toward our eternal future. Our present circumstances, relationships, and experiences are to be viewed with the bigger picture in mind. That is, what we focus our attention on should be of lasting value. Let's not waste our energy on what temporarily satisfies and has no guarantees. God says that we tap into His supernatural kingdom by faith and not by sight (2 Corinthians 5:7). Working toward selfish gain is of no value. We may have decisions we need to make based on this fact. God promises according to 1 Corinthians 15:58 that if we give ourselves fully to His work, our labor is not in vain. That means whatever we do for Him earns us eternal rewards.

Do you sense that God may be leading you to remove yourself from a particular circumstance or person(s)? If so, know that you are not alone. God has promised His Holy Spirit to empower and strengthen you for the task.

Let's pray:

Dear heavenly Father, Your Word is full of treasures. Thank You for revealing Yourself to me through Your Word. I know that I am a stranger in this present world—I am just passing through. I pray that my eyes will be fixed on the unseen reality of Your kingdom. I want to live by faith not by sight. "Your kingdom come, Your will be done on earth as it is in heaven." In Jesus' name I pray, Amen.

DAY 2: ORDAINED DAYS

Today's Scripture:

All the days ordained for me were written in your book before one of them came to be.
Psalm 139:16

The births of my three daughters were and probably will always be my favorite times in life. To literally give birth to new life is miraculous and unexplainable. The feelings that accompany the birth of a child are overwhelmingly filled with love. I truly did not know I had the capacity to love that deeply. When I was pregnant, I did all I could to ensure a healthy baby being formed in my womb. I ate properly, took prenatal vitamins, visited the doctor, rested, exercised, and prayed. Not once did I wake up and say, "Okay, today I will make my baby's fingers and toes." I was not in control of that part of the pregnancy—God was. To me, that was part of the miracle of birth. My girls were born so perfect. They all had two eyes in the right places, two ears, a nose, beautiful mouth, and a perfect little body that was so precious to cuddle. The miracle was that I didn't create or make this beautiful baby within me. Yes, I had a part in the conception, but not the formation. I had such mixed feelings when I would bring my babies home from the hospital. They were so perfectly formed; I didn't want anything or anyone to take away from their perfect little bodies. I knew they were born sinful in spirit, but physically they were beautiful and flawless.

I didn't get to pick who my children would be or what they would look like. This was God's plan in my life as He designed a baby in my womb. My children are a gift to me from the Lord. Neither did they get to choose who their parents would be. All of this was ordained by God.

Think about your own birth. In the space below, write the circumstances surrounding your birth. Include your parents, your birth order, where you were born, and any world or family events occurring simultaneously.

I was born in Newton. Mes parents
savait que j'était une fille. Mes deux
parents it dient la . Je suis arrive et
3 jours en ret
arc ...

We may not be able to control what we look like, who our family is, when we were born, or the circumstances surrounding our birth, but we can see a glimpse of God's involvement. Read each of the following Scriptures and describe what God's involvement is in the very beginning of your life.

Psalm 139:13-16:

He made us in our mother womb. Nothing that he didn't no. He knew how many days we was gonna have. Were

Jeremiah 1:5:

He chose us for something. He knew us. He made us to speak for the people

Acts 17:26, 27:

He is not to us. He created all. He fixed the seasons...

As you read the above Scriptures, did you grasp the time and thought your Creator has already invested in you? You certainly were not an accident. No matter the circumstances of your birth, you were born exactly when and how God had already planned. He is the Master Planner, Creator, Maker, and Inventor of your very being. What was your favorite part among the Scriptures above?

He chose us for something (whatever it is).

I want you to understand fully that God has a plan for your past, your present, and your future. If He planned for you to be born, then He has a plan for you to live life to the fullest in this generation. He has created you to live among this generation, not only to know Him but also to make Him known. God has called and equipped you to face these specific temptations of your generation. He knows you can be the winner in every situation.

What encouragement can you gain from 1 Corinthians 15:57?

God gave us victory

Esther's Example

Esther was a godly, young woman who fearfully lived to fulfill her God–given destiny.
She knew God and made Him known among her generation and generations to come.
Esther was a Jew who was chosen to be married to a Persian king. Jews followed God;
Persians followed their earthly king. The Jews were looked down upon because of their
beliefs, and some Persians even wanted them dead. According to Esther 8:5,6 what
request did Esther make to the king?

*She asked the king to don't do
what Haman wanted to do (kill
the jews) but & to let the jews safe-*

What did the king do in response to her request? Look at Esther 8:11.

*He wrote "Every Jews on t's day
can kill, destruct, keep everything
from the others even - all ladie and
The children*

Just as Esther rose up and became all God wanted her to be and do, so you, too, can
be and do all God has for you. Let the words spoken over Esther speak over you today.
Fill in the words of Esther 4:14b. "And who knows but that _____ have
come to _____ _____ for such a _____ as this?"
Yes, Princess, you have come to a royal position as daughter of the King for such a
time as now. Just as God appointed Esther and Jeremiah and many others in the Old

*C'est peut-être [...] situation [...]
[...] à [...] tu [...] venue [...]*

54

and New Testaments, so He appoints you to fulfill a unique role in this present age. He appoints you within your family, your school, your job, your neighborhood, and your church.

In the physical realm, Queen Esther and the Jews had enemies who wanted to kill them. In the spiritual realm, we, as believers, have an enemy who desires that we do not live out our calling in Christ. Our enemy, Satan, has a plan to destroy our self-esteem, our confidence, our reputation, and our hope of ever being who we are meant to be in Christ. We shouldn't believe the lies from Satan about ourselves. Let's know the truth about who we are, and then live out that truth in our daily lives even as we face temptations.

Write the words of John 10:10.

"Le voleur vient seulement pour voler tuer et détruire. Moi je suis venu pour que les gens dient la vie, et pour que cette vie soit abondante."

Let's pray:

Dear heavenly Father, You have come to give me life by sending Your Son, Jesus who is the Resurrection and the Life. I acknowledge that I do have an enemy who does not want me to be all I can be for You. I choose not to listen to the voice of my enemy, but to listen to Your voice that speaks only truth and life. Thank You for my life. Thank You for my life in You. In Jesus' name I pray, Amen.

Day 3: Meditate On It

Today's Scripture:

This Book of the Law shall not depart out of your mouth, but you shall meditate on it day and night, that you may observe and do according to all that is written in it. For then you shall make your way prosperous, and then you shall deal wisely and have good success Joshua 1:8 (AMP).

Yesterday we learned that God had a plan for our lives even before we were born. We learned that what God has called us to do fits perfectly with the needs of this generation. We may sometimes feel as if we would be happier or easier if we had lived in the 1900s or 1950s or a future time, but that's not the truth. God has ordained for you and me to occupy our states and our cities now for His glory and our satisfaction. I understand that many of you are in search of your specific, unique purpose. Or maybe some of you do have a clear passion and direction for your life, but you're in the waiting process. You have to keep in mind that God wants to fulfill His purposes for your life just as much, or even more, than you do. You bring Him pleasure when you obey in small and big ways. So what do we do until God either reveals our purpose or provides opportunities to serve Him through our passions? We wait.

Write in your own words what Joshua 1:8 commands of us.

He commands us to say and repeat Gods rules day and night

What is the promise associated with this command?

That everything we are gonna do will have success

56

Joshua 1:8 is part of God's instruction to Joshua before he fulfilled his destiny of leading God's people into the Promised Land. We can know that God desires for us to obey this command because it is a common theme throughout both the Old and New Testaments.

Look up the following verses and write how they are similar to the command given in Joshua 1:8:

~~Gods rules everyething~~

Psalm 1:2:

Gods rules everyday and night

Psalm 119:14-16:

I'm gonna obey to ryourrules, not gonna forget it

James 1:25:

Study gods words, listen, dont forget

The Hebrew word for *meditate* is *hagah* which means "to utter a sound." We normally tend to think that meditating means to think or reflect in our hearts and minds; in other words, to do it silently. Silently is not what the Lord is commanding us to do. He says that His Word is to keep coming from our mouths and *to utter a sound* (meditate) on it. God wants us to read it out loud even when we are by ourselves. Exodus 13:9 says that "the Law of the Lord is to be on your lips." I think God is trying to tell us something about living life to the fullest where we will be "prosperous and successful." When we speak God's Word out loud we are more conscience of it in our minds and hearts. When we read God's Word out loud our ears hear it spoken, and therefore we receive His words through external means as well as internal. God's Word penetrates our being in a much more powerful way than if we just read it silently. It is the same thing with your school work. If you write or say out loud what you are studying, you learn quicker and remember better.

Reading God's Word aloud during your study times alone with Him may seem awkward at first, but I challenge you to put it into practice today and see the difference it makes. Reading out loud is no different than talking on the phone to someone. No one else in the room can hear the person on the other line, but you can, and you respond out loud to the person. Read back God's Word to Him and hear Him speak over you through the written word and through the Holy Spirit within you.

The rest of the verse in Joshua 1:8 says that we are to "do according to all that is written in it." That is the toughest part, huh? It is just difficult at times because we still have our fleshly side that usually wants what is contrary to God's Word.

List some things that help you to "do" according to God's Word. For instance: listening to Christian music.

listen to christian music, repeat it, listen to oder people that believes in Christ and speak about him ...

Keep doing those things. According to John 14:26 what is a job of the Holy Spirit?

He helps us, will us what Jesus said, teach us ...

All You Can Be

So, what does Joshua 1:8 have to do with our purposes and callings upon our lives? Everything. How can we ever know the will of God if we are not in His Word everyday? We can not. If you desire to be prosperous and successful in this generation, you have to have a plan and be deliberate about following it. The number one thing you can do to fulfill your destiny is to have a continuing relationship with God by reading His Word out loud and by doing what He is sweetly telling you to do. I believe that before you can be all God wants you to be in your future occupation and as a future wife and mother, you have to be all He wants you to be today.

The summer before my senior year of high school, I felt the Lord calling me into full-time ministry. At that time, I did not know what women did in full-time ministry. I knew some worked with children, but that was not me. I surrendered to full-time ministry without a clue as to what He saw in me that would qualify me to be in ministry. I can not sing. I am not an athlete. I knew I could not pastor. I did not know any women Bible teachers or speakers. And, I did not know I had a heart to write.

I went to a Christian university where I took a couple of ministry classes. I soon realized that a ministry degree was not a piece of the puzzle as I searched for what He wanted me to do in ministry. I graduated with a degree to teach Physical Education K-12. A week after graduation, I married Richard Johnson who graduated with a degree in ministry specializing in youth. Aha! Had the Lord called me to full-time ministry because I would marry a minister? As the years went by, I knew the Lord had something else in store for me personally in ministry. I was 17 when I surrendered to the ministry. As I write, I have lived another 17 years, and I am just now fulfilling what I believed He called me to do that summer before my senior year. I pray none of you will have to wait 17 years. But if you do, "Be very careful, then, how you live—not as

unwise but as wise, making the most of every opportunity, because the days are evil,"
(Ephesians 5:15,16).

It is your turn to write out a prayer to your heavenly Father. You can use Psalm 19:14
as a guide to your prayer. "May the words of my mouth and the meditation of my heart
be pleasing in your sight, O LORD, my Rock and my Redeemer."

*Seigneur, faite ce que je dise ou passe
soit comme tu le veus. Merci car tu
est mon rocher et mon défenseur. Aide
moi dans tout ce que je
fais pour toi. Au nom de Jesus
Amen*

DAY 4: A WARNING

Today's Scripture:

By them is your servant warned; in keeping them there is great reward.
Psalm 19:11

Let's first look at the context of today's Scripture verse. Read Psalm 19:7-11.

These verses describe God's Holy Word. David, the psalmist, describes the different
aspects of God's written Word. He uses words such as "law," "statutes," "precepts,"
and "commands" to show the variety of ways God's Word pertains to our Christian life.
Write all the different adjectives and phrases David used to portray God's Holy Word
from Psalm 19:7-10. (Verse 7 has already been done for you as an example.)

"perfect, reviving the soul"

"give wisdom", "give happy heart", "light "to see", "respect "the Lord", "pretty things", "Valables", "true", "better than gold", "better than honey".

These adjectives and phrases describing God's Word speak freedom to my soul. When I open up the Bible during my quiet times or as I am led through a sermon or message, I know that I will find words that are true and good for me. Sometimes, I may not necessarily want to hear what I am reading, but I can trust God to know that what He is commanding me to do is good for me.

Read Psalm 19:11. In this verse we are told that God's Word warns us, and that if we not only hear God's Word, but also do it – we will be rewarded. James 1:22-25 emphasizes this truth as well. In your own words, write what you believe God desires us to know through James 1:22-25.

"reject" all bad things and recieve God's words to save our lifes"

Rockin' Rewards

Remember Joshua 1:8 from yesterday's study? It told us that by obeying God's Word we will find success and prosperity. Psalm 19:11 tells us we will have a reward. James 1:25 says we will be blessed when we do God's Word. Are those not enough reasons for us to know the Bible and do what it says? But, then, why is it so hard sometimes do according to the Bible? List some reasons why you find it hard to do what God commands. (I want you to write about you personally—not why you think it is hard for someone else.)

"Because others will laugh thing at us", "if it's something hard", "if it's not like we do everyday"

It is important to understand that when we hear the words "success and prosperity" we know that does not mean popularity and fat bank accounts. God does allow some people to experience earthly success at school, work, etc. God also allows some people to make a larger salary. But these are not indicators of one's obedience to God. Yes, God does reward the obedient, and often the earthly rewards are different for different people . . . and always are used for HIS GLORY. But you can be sure He will reward you with SPIRITUAL success and prosperity such as eternal life, access to Him 24/7, the Holy Spirit, joy, peace, and the list goes on.

Thank you for being honest. It is my turn to be honest. Sometimes I have a hard time doing what God is telling me because I have an authority problem. I want to be the boss of my own life and make up my own rules. Can you relate? For some of us who are more prone to stubbornness, authority can be a problem. If you're still living with your parents or when you did live with your parents, did you ever dream about the day that you could do whatever you wanted? Wake up when you want to. Eat what you want. Go places and be home at any time. Be with whom you want.

There are many decisions we have to make every day from what to wear to what to do with free time. When we live at home, our parents usually have a say in most of these decisions. As we grow-up and move out of the house, we are much more responsible for our daily decisions. Even though our parents or guardians may not be present in our day-to-day lives, we need to realize that we are not and never will be our own boss. So, with freedom comes responsibility. Since we are not our own boss, and yet have the responsibility to make specific, little and big decisions, what should we know? I think we need to know that just because we are princesses does not mean that we can get away with sinning. The Bible says in James 4:17 (NASB) "To one who knows the right thing to do and yet does not do it, to him it is sin." We will sin. We will, unfortunately, do things or say things that are not pleasing to God. We should not continue in our sin. Look at a passage of Scripture that serves as a warning for us as daughters of the King. Look up and read Isaiah 30:8-21 and answer the following questions.

How did God describe His children in verse 9?

desobeying people, doesn't listen to God words"/ liers"...

What did God's children want from their religious teachers according to verses 10,11?

Don't tell the true"/ "Tell good things even if it's not true"/ leave the right way"/ "Don't talk about God".

What do you think God was saying about their sin in verses 12-14?

"You rejecte my words"/ "This fault is gonna be for you"/ "You don't even serve for Something".

What would God's people have none of according to verse 15?

"You will be saved only if you turn to me, Slow down, trust me"/ But he did't wat to".

Fill in the blanks of verse 18.

"Yet the LORD _waits_ to be _the time_ to _show_ ; he _waits_ to
show _his_ compassion. For the LORD is a God of justice. _Happy_ are
those who _waits_ for him."

I hope you sensed the love in God's words in verse 18. He longs—He waits expectantly
to be gracious to YOU! God wants to forgive you and wash you and cleanse you and put
a smile back on your face. Your God "rises"—He actively does something for you. He
doesn't just say "you're forgiven." He acts on His grace. God may give you a verse to
minister to your particular need. He may give you a song to sing. He may use someone
else to send you a word of encouragement. He may tenderly speak to your heart. Wait
for Him. Do not give up on Him. Do not believe the lie that God is not there for you.

No matter how you feel you have messed up or sinned too much, God still longs to be gracious to you. Listen to Him. Listen to the spiritual leaders God has placed in your life. He is worth it! He thinks you are worth it too!

Let's pray:

Dear heavenly Father, I come before you with my deepest emotions and thoughts that I don't want anyone to know—You hear me, really hear me. You desire to hold me, to rock me in Your embrace. You are my Rock. You hide me in the cleft of the Rock which is You. You rescue me and silence my enemies. You tell me the Truth. You wipe my tears and put a smile on my face. You lift my head as I gaze into Your life-changing eyes of You where I find rest for my weary soul. I love You. In Jesus' name I pray. Amen.

Day 5: The Sure Foundation

Today's Scripture:

He will be the sure foundation for your times, a rich store of salvation and wisdom and knowledge; the fear of the Lord is the key to this treasure.
Isaiah 33:6

In the college Sunday School class I co-teach, the other teacher drew a tree on the dry-erase board asking us to list things/actions that serve as "roots" in our spiritual lives. The teacher wanted to make the point that the "duties" or disciplines we do make a difference in our growth as a believer just as tree roots affect the growth and health of the tree.

Check all the spiritual disciplines you have participated in or are currently participating in.

☑ prayer ☐ personal Bible reading ☐ singing to God ☐ doing a Bible study ☐ going to church ☐ fellowship with other believers ☑ listening to Christian music ☐ attending a small accountability group ☐ participating in local mission projects ☐ going on a mission trip ☐ mentoring (either by someone or to someone) ☐ attend spiritual retreats

In what ways do the spiritual disciplines you checked provide spiritual growth in your personal life?

I have Christian Parents

What is your motivation for doing those disciplines?

Because God want me to do that Because it's good!

What do you hope will be the outcome of continuing to participate in those disciplines?

Be more and more like Jesus, feeling good, learn more...

How much time do you spend per day devoted to God whether in thought or deed?

40 - 45 minutes

I hope you put some thought into answering the questions above. I sure do not want you to feel condemned or belittled in any way. I just want you to do a little soul searching in regard to your devotion to God and in your pursuit of Him. Sometimes, we just need to stop and examine where we have been, and then decide if we need to keep going in the same manner or switch directions a bit. One thing I pray that you will gain from participating in this Bible study (which, by the way, I am extremely proud of you for getting this far) is a deepening hunger and thirst for the one and only, your King, and true lover of your soul.

If we are really going to mature spiritually, we cannot just go through the motions in our spiritual disciplines. I believe we must want Him—not just what He can give us, not just so we can "look good," not just so we can check off something to say we did it, and not just because it is expected of us.

Carefully and slowly read out loud Isaiah 55:1-3.

According to verse 1, how many times does God say the word *come*?

3 times

Do you sense His invitation to you? Do you feel wanted by Him? Express your emotions as you consider His invitation.

Yes, Yes. He call us and loves us and that shows us how he is great. This makes us feel glad.

What do you think God wants us to think about from verse 2?

That he feeds us with his words. Nothing other can do that. We have to listen to him.

God knows that we desire to be full, not empty. God knows we have desires that are unfulfilled. According to the rest of verse 2, God wants to give us the best of the best.

66

He tells us where to find the best, the place of abundance in verse 3. Fill in the blanks of 3a. "Give ear and come to _me_ ; hear _me_ , that your soul may live."

God wants us to want Him. God is the "me" in this verse. He is the source of all the satisfaction we could ever need.

Read Isaiah 55:6. What two actions do we need to take in finding the Lord?

Look for him, and call him

Seeking the Lord and calling upon Him are what I hope you are doing as you do your spiritual disciplines. The Lord is our God who wants us to find Him and thoroughly enjoy Him!

I asked you earlier what you hope will be the outcome of continuing to participate in your spiritual disciplines. I understand that sometimes you may feel like you are not as spiritual as you would like to be, and that you have a long way to go. I want to encourage you today and give you the little push you need to keep on keeping on. I hope you find encouragement in these next Scriptures. Read and dwell on Matthew 7:24-27.

What is the main difference between the wise man and the foolish man?

One build his house upon the rock and the other upon the sand

The wise man and the foolish man both heard God's words, but it was the foolish man who did not obey them—he did not live out what he knew to be the truth.

So…it is true! It is not just Sunday School mumbo jumbo. When the winds of change, the storms of life and the earthquakes that shake everything you know come to pass, if your heart and mind have a foundation based on your relationship with the Lord—you can make it. You can stand firm and overcome your circumstances.

This is the time in your life when you are building the layers of your foundation or "roots" of who you are and what you believe. Take every opportunity to participate in Bible studies, mission trips, conferences, retreats, Sunday School, Wednesday night services, and most important your personal quiet times. You may think life is okay, and that you do not "need" God now because your life is going smoothly. That's a lie from the enemy and a plan to make sure in the future when something unexpected happens, you fail, you give up, or you fall. Do all you can now while you are young to build a solid foundation in your inner being because you have no idea what will happen tomorrow. You may think you have your life all planned out. It's good to make goals and to think about your future, but really no one can guarantee your plans will come to pass. If you want to invest in your future and plan for success, it isn't in your education, your diet, who your parents are, where you work, or who your boyfriend is. It's what you are doing by investing yourself in your personal relationship with your heavenly King.

What is so awesome about having a personal walk with the Lord is that He takes care of our education, diet, job, parents, boyfriend, and so much more. He gives us wisdom and discernment to make good decisions that give us a future and life and hope. Write out Matthew 6:33: *Cherchez d'abord le royaume de Dieu et ce que Dieu demande. Il vous*

Reread the Scripture verse for today. *donnera le reste en plus*

For our prayer today, pray Psalm 63 out loud and with a fresh wave of passion for God alone.

WEEK 4

ABOUNDING IN LOVE

DAY 1: As Yourself

Today's Scripture:

And the second is like it; "Love your neighbor as yourself."
Matthew 22:39

My mind is flooded with so many thoughts associated with this week's subject: love. My mind is also on you. I am burdened for you and your generation. I am deeply concerned about the self-hate I have observed in middle school, high school, and college girls. Girls who battle self-hate come from a variety of families—close, dysfunctional, and somewhere in between. A trend associated with self-hate is cutting. Cutting is when a girl uses a razor blade (or other sharp object) to secretly cut the inside part of the forearms, back of the thighs, or someplace on her body that is not seen obviously. Another form of self-hate is anorexia when an adequate amount of food is not consumed and exercise is obsessive. Another form of self-hate is the way a girl talks about herself. She expresses self-hate as she consistently and continually says negative things about the way she looks, what she can not do right, and what she wishes she could change about herself.

Can you name another destructive behavior girls do because of self-hate?

boulimie, colère, pensée negative, dépression...

To add to the list I would like to include: smoking, drugs, promiscuity, shop-lifting, drinking, overspending, overeating, pulling out hair, biting nails, bulimia, and thinking suicidal thoughts.

Do you or have you battled with a particular destructive behavior? If so, briefly describe your battle.

Not, really. No.

Princess, I need you to know that these destructive behaviors are a serious problem. I believe God takes them very seriously. I also need you to know that I understand and so does God. I'm aware that you do not like what you are doing and yet you do not know how to stop. What scares me is that some of you have been participating in the destructive behavior for months and even years without anyone knowing. This behavior has become routine and seems non-threatening since you have been able to "get away with it." I pray that today's lesson either will be a wake-up call or a warning.

What one thing do the following verses have in common?
Isaiah 44:20, Jeremiah 7:8, Jeremiah 8:5

Croire des choses fausses.

Your generation is experiencing self-hate, which is something the Israelites also experienced. The LORD said about the Israelites, "Are they not rather harming themselves, to their own shame?" (Jeremiah 7:19). Isaiah and Jeremiah were used of God to tell God's people that He sees what they are doing. The Israelites were told to listen to God and obey what He had already instructed them. The above verses told us that the Israelites were trusting in a lie. I believe those involved in a destructive behavior also believe a lie about themselves and their future. This lie may be obvious or it may be buried deeply in the subconscious.

What does God say will happen to those who refuse to listen to the truth according to Jeremiah 6:19?

Faire venir le malheur

I know these words from Jeremiah can be hard to hear. It is important for us to know the consequences to our disobedience. God says we will bear the fruit of our destructive ways. A New Testament principle says the same thing in Galatians 6:7, "Do not be deceived: God cannot be mocked. A man reaps what he sows." We are warned to look at the path we are heading down. If we take a long, serious look, we can see that literal death is at the end of most destructive behaviors.

Naming the Enemy

What does John 10:10 say about Satan?

Le voleur vient pour voler tuer et détruire

71

Through the destructive behavior, Satan's plan is to destroy your self-worth, healthy love of yourself, witness to others, reputation, and ability to love others. He seeks to steal your confidence, purity, innocence, joy, hope, and peace. He is seeking to kill your love for God, your pursuit of righteousness, God's plan for your life, and even your very life. Satan is lying to you and you may not even know it. His ways are very subtle, crafty, and hard to recognize. Before long you are caught in an unhealthy addiction that is causing harm either emotionally, physically, socially, sexually, or financially. You begin to feel trapped. Examples of some lies you may believe if you struggle with "cutting" are: "I can't do anything right"; "Nobody loves me or even notices me"; or "I am not a good person."   Examples of some lies you may be believing if you struggle with anorexia are: "I am too fat"; "If I were only thinner then I would be more liked"; "No one has as much fat as I do"; or "How could anyone love me with all this fat on me?" These are lies Satan wants you to believe as truth, and he unfortunately can be very convincing.

List some other lies associated with a specific destructive behavior.

drugs : ne pas se sentir bien dans sa peau Penser : "Cela va me faire oublier"; "Au moins c'est quelque chose qui me défend"...

Write Romans 1:25:

"Ils ont remplacé le vrai Dieu par des faux dieux ils sont adoré et ils ont servi Ce que Dieu a créer à la place du créateur! La ange à lui p... toujours! Amen!"

You may feel trapped, helpless, and hopeless. Those feelings may be what you are feeling now, but in Christ you have a beautiful future. Now is the time to expose the lie you have believed. Cry out to Jesus and ask Him to show you the lie and where it originated (in other words—who told you the lie—parents, friend, or boyfriend?). When you know the specific lie, confess it to God and tell Him you are sorry for believing it and that you will no longer accept this lie as truth. Also, it may be important to talk to someone who is older and wiser in the Scriptures. Please consider confiding in a Sunday School teacher, professional counselor, or mentor who can daily encourage you through this battle. This may be one of the hardest things you have ever done. Satan will try to convince you that you still "need" the behavior. He will also try to get you to do it "one more time," hoping that you will never stop. This battle will cause you to have to fight for what is rightfully yours—abundant life (John 10:10). From one who has fought and overcome—God is with you every step of the way and will lead you to victory and rest.

In conclusion and for our prayer today, please read out loud and receive in your heart these beautiful words your heavenly Father speaks over you even as He spoke over the Israelites who also needed hope and restoration.

Let's pray:

Read aloud the following Scripture as your prayer today. Jeremiah 33: 6-9:
"Nevertheless, I will bring health and healing to it; I will heal my people and will let them enjoy abundant peace and security. I will bring Judah and Israel back from captivity and will rebuild them as they were before. I will cleanse them from all the sin they have committed against me and will forgive all their sins of rebellion against me. Then this city (you) will bring me renown, joy, praise and honor before all nations on earth that hear of all the good things I do for it; and they will be in awe and will tremble at the abundant prosperity and peace I provide for it."

Day 2: Your Love

Today's Scripture:

And this is my prayer: that your love may abound more and more in knowledge and depth of insight, so that you may be able to discern what is best and may be pure and blameless until the day of Christ.

Philippians 1:9-10

Sometimes I do not even have to know a girl to recognize by her countenance that she is searching and struggling to know who she is and to like herself. Some, though, masquerade it all too well. Those who "masquerade" are the ones who give every outward appearance they are "fine," but inwardly they wonder how much longer they can keep this game in play. For all who battle some form of self-hate, life can be like a roller coaster ride with many ups and downs and unexpected turns. It is time to stop the ride, get off, and live life as a princess in Christ. Our Prince of Peace will take us for the best ride of our lives with our hands and heads lifted high to the sky!

Yesterday's Scripture verse for the day is the second greatest commandment.
Write Matthew 22:39.

Et voici le 2ème commandement puis est aussi important que le 1er. Tu dois aimer ton prochain comme toi même

This command sounds so simplistic, and yet it is exactly what Satan does not want us to do. Satan doesn't want us to love ourselves or love those with whom we have relationships.

What do you think Satan wants to accomplish by lying to us to get us not to love ourselves?

He wants us feel bad and sad. Not good.

If we don't love ourselves, how does that affect our love for others?

We don't like the others. Because we are sad because we don't like ourselves.

One of Satan's goals, while he still has the time (Revelation 12:12), is to make God look bad, look like a fraud, or look little. Satan does this by attacking those who call themselves Christians. For those of us who call God our Lord, Satan desires to kill, steal, and destroy so God cannot be glorified through the Christian.

Fill in the blanks to John 13:35:

"By this ____all____ _____ will know that you are my disciples, if you ___love___ one another."

for

Just Like Her

A trap that Satan uses very early in life is the sin of comparison. When we compare ourselves to other girls we have neither the time nor desire to love them in a godly manner. As girls we compare our physical appearance to other girls' physical appearance. We are quick at it too. We can estimate her dress size, weight, social status, and cuteness all in a matter of seconds. Why do we do this to one another?! I am just as guilty as anyone. Unfortunately I became a "pro" at this because I believed the lie that the thinnest and prettiest was the "better person." I am so sorry I fell for that lie. Because of my own insecurities, I compared myself to other girls so I could somehow feel better about myself. Of course, it never worked. I always came away feeling worse about myself because there was always someone thinner and prettier. The worst thing about all this mental comparison is that it distracts us from our true value and service to God. We become so busy thinking negatively about ourselves that we miss an opportunity to hear from God and to see a way to bless someone with our words or actions.

Is this "hitting home" to you in any way? Can you remember a moment when you got caught up in the sin of comparison and ended up feeling worse about yourself?

Yes, when a girl older than me was beauty I thought I was horible. When I am with her. Or when boys say things...

Where do our standards of physical appearance come from? Are they coming from the latest magazines or the Word of God? The magazines in the stores are full of lies and disillusions. The writers and editors of the magazines do not really care about our self-worth or self-esteem even though they have an appearance of caring. All the magazines really care about is making money. If they really cared about us, we would feel better after reading the magazines.

God loves us so much. We cannot measure God's love for us. His love is abounding; it overflows with much to spare. A question I frequently ask my daughters is "Who loves you the most?" They say, "Jesus!" It is true for you too—Jesus loves you the most. What does God lovingly want you to know through these Scriptures?

Write what you hear Him speaking as you read the following verses:

1 Samuel 16:7:

"Don't care about it" "I don't see like people" "People look to what they see outside but i look in the heart"

Proverbs 31:30:

"la beaulé ne dure pas" "Le femme qui respecte le Saigneur est digne de louange"

Luke 16:15:

"Dieu regarde au coeur" Ce qui est important pour les hommes est horrible pour Dieu"

1 Peter 3:3, 4:

"Votre beauté ne doit pas être extérieure" "Cette beauté doit être à l'intérieure de nous et elle ne disparaît pas"

When you look into your full-length mirror, please accept every part of your body from head to toe. In fact, you can do this verbally by telling God you accept your eyes, nose, hair, etc. . . This is a powerful tool that keeps Satan away from attacking your thoughts about your beautifully created body. Would you do me a huge favor? For our prayer today, would you please go right now to your full-length mirror and talk to Jesus. Tell Him that you accept every part of your body, even what you dislike. I know this seems awkward. I have done it recently and can honestly tell a difference in my perspective of my body. I do—I actually like my body—that is why I am encouraging you to do the same. No more delays, you and Jesus go have a talk. Again, I am so proud of you!

Day 3: New Day

Today's Scripture:

The LORD within her is righteous; he does no wrong. Morning by morning he dispenses

his justice, and every new day he does not fail, yet the unrighteous know no shame.

Zephaniah 3:5

Overcoming bad habits of self-hate takes time and deliberate work to break free of any

destructive behavior. What I do believe is that because we have bravely opened our

hearts to God and recognized sinful patterns in our lives, we are on the right road that

leads to abundant life in Christ. We are beginning a new day today. Say this out loud:

"Today is a new day!" Go ahead, say it again! We have something to celebrate.

Fill in the blanks to Isaiah 43:18-19 "Forget the ___*old past*___ things: do not dwell on

the ___*before*___ . See, ___*I'm*___ ___*gonna*___ doing a ___*new*___ thing!

_____ it springs up; do you not perceive it? ___*Open the way*___

making a way in the desert and streams in the wasteland."

We celebrate that God, the "I AM THAT I AM" (Exodus 3:14, KJV), will do a new thing

in us now—today if we let Him.

You may have made mistakes—small or big—but God can redeem all of that. In order

for His plan to be fulfilled in your unique life, you need to cooperate. You can cooperate

with His plan by making a decision to stop doing what is destructive. Your decision

may be to stop comparing yourself to others, stop smoking, or stop giving in to sexual

compulsions. Whatever yours may be, let us make a commitment together to stop the

destructive behavior.

I, _Emma_ , commit this day _10/11/12_ to stop _Comparing my self to others_ .

(your name)   (today's date)   (destructive behavior)

I know . . . I know . . . Easier said than done!

You may have tried in the past to stop only to start again. Frustrating, huh? I pray

today's commitment will be different because you will learn to depend on your King in a

way you never have.

There are two things I want you to know:

1. We can not stop the destructive behavior on our own.

Look up the following verses and state the overall message.

Psalm 14:2, 3, Psalm 51:5, Jeremiah 13:23

① Le Seigneur regarde sur la terre mais aucun
n'était pas pecheur; était comme lui
② Quelqu'un reconnaît qu'il est pecheur
③ Le Seigneur dit que le peut agit mal, et qu'il ne peut pas agir bien.

According to these verses, why is it impossible for us to stop the destructive behavior

on our own?

Because we need god's love and help.
It's to hard for us because we are sinners.

That's right. We were not created to help ourselves. We are in desperate need of a

Savior. Jesus is our Savior who saved us from eternal punishment at the time of our

salvation, and He is also the one who continues to save us as we cry out to Him

(Psalm 50:15).

What is Jesus' promise in Matthew 19:26?

"Pour les hommes c'est impossible mais pour Dieu tout est possible".

2. We can stop the destructive behavior through God in us.

According to today's verse Zephaniah 3:5 where is the LORD and what is He?

He is evrywhere despenses his justice, he does no wrong he is righteous

We can only be good and do good because of Him who lives in us as believers in Jesus Christ.

What do you learn from Romans 4:25 and Romans 5:19?

à cause de nos pechés.

① Jesus a été livrer, mais Dieu l'a reveillé de la mort pour nous rendre justes"

pecheur

② Explique que par l'homme avant plusieurs ho-mmes etait rendus pecheur et l'homme à déci un grand⊀

⊀nombre seront justes —

In Week 1 we studied in detail what God did for us by sending Jesus to die for our sins who rose from the dead so we, too, can have eternal life with Him. God has declared us righteous, holy, and innocent, which is the meaning of *justification*. Because Christ dwells within us, God declares us holy and free from sin. To break free from our sinful habits, we need to see ourselves as God does and to call upon His power in us to help us stop the destructive behavior. Ephesians 3:20 tells us His power is at work within us for His glory. It is time to see His power at work in your life. You may experience His power through:

- A professional counselor
- A student pastor
- A rehabilitation center
- A friend
- Memorizing Scripture
- Laying on of hands and prayer
- Reaching out to others in need

All of these are ways God can show His power, but of course, I am not one to limit Him. The most important thing is to stay in God's Word and to pray, pray, and pray some more. As we pray and read the Bible, He will direct us to our place of freedom from sin. The psalmist prayed, "You are good, and what You do is good; teach me your decrees" (Psalm 119:68).

Recently I was reading in my bedroom in a chair that allows me to see down the hallway. My youngest daughter was playing in her room with her door opened. She would come out into the hallway still playing but also keeping an eye on me. She would say a few words to me and I would respond. She continued this for about 15 minutes. Then, without hesitation she stopped playing and crawled into my lap. She had her sweet pajamas on, and I pulled my arms around her and held her close. I told her that when she was a baby, every night I would rock her to sleep with her head on my chest. She remembered that I would also sing to her. She said, "Mommy, sing every song you can think of." She snuggled close to me and listened as I sang simple praise songs to Jesus. I then felt the presence of the Lord with us. I felt Him impress me that He waits for us as His children to crawl into His lap (Luke 13:34). He sits and watches us as we hurriedly and busily go about our daily duties. Sure, we may offer up a short prayer in which God responds, but He does have more for us. More. We still need the comfort of His strong arms around us to quiet and calm us. He, too, sings love songs over us (Zephaniah 3:17). He doesn't force us into His lap. He waits patiently for us to want to be with Him. Just as my 6 year old still needs my embrace, we, too, desperately need God's embrace to strengthen us and to give us hope. I did not have to ask my daughter to sit with me. She came voluntarily and received my love I so willingly had to give.

Let's pray:

Dear heavenly Father, "May your unfailing love be my comfort, according to your promise to your servant" (Psalm 119:76). In Jesus' name I pray, Amen.

Day 4: Love / Hate Relationship

Today's Scripture:

You love those who hate you and hate those who love you.
2 Samuel 19:6

"The enemy makes sure many obstacles stand in the way of the liberated life in Christ. No one is more effective for the Kingdom than the subject who is truly free to testify and serve."

– Beth Moore,
Breaking Free

Satan strongly opposes our fight to be free of our battle with self-hate. Satan wants us to continue believing lies about ourselves and our future because he knows that once we become free we will be a threat to his kingdom of darkness. When we live out our true identity in Christ—royal by blood—we bring glory to our King. Isaiah 61:3 says that we will become a "display of his splendor."

A Greater Victory

Fascinating events are recorded in 2 Samuel 13-19 about King David and two of his sons. We don't have the opportunity to study the story in detail, but I do want to highlight a conversation David had with his appointed chief commanding officer, Joab. Let me give some background to the conversation. King David was in a time of rest with foreign enemies, so he was at home for several years. Unfortunately, David was not active in the lives of his children. Because of his lack of parenting, many problems existed. His eldest son, Amnon, raped his sister Tamar. David's second-born son, Absalom, wanted David to avenge the rape. David did nothing. So, Absalom killed Amnon. Absalom harbored bitterness and hatred toward his father. The two did not see or talk to one another for 3 years after the murder. David then had Absalom come back to Jerusalem, but the two only reunited and did not reconcile. While Absalom remained in Jerusalem for 4 years he deceived the people of Israel who were under the leadership of King David by telling them that the king could not do anything about their problems. Absalom stole the hearts of the people and wanted to be king in place of his father. Absalom got an army of men and plotted to attack and kill David and his men. David soon found out that his enemy was his own son. In the end David and his men won the battle and Absalom was killed. David grieved deeply over the death of his son. Yes, he had reason to grieve, but realistically he had a greater reason to rejoice because his enemy was dead, and he would continue to rule the Israelites as God had ordained.

Now, please read 2 Samuel 19:1-8. In your own words what did Joab need David to know (verses 5-6)?

That the soldiers saved his life and his family.

I think it is fair to say that at this point in David's life he was an emotional basket case. He was not in a position emotionally to think clearly, so he was wise to listen to his chief officer.

Look again at 2 Samuel 19:6. The original Hebrew word for *love* is *ahab* which means "to have affection for." It is not true "love" in the sense that this particular use of the word *love* does not mean the same as in other Scriptures like 1 Corinthians 13. The King James Version of 2 Samuel 19:6 says, "In that thou lovest thine enemies and hatest thy friends."

Could this verse apply to you? Do you find some comfort in your destructive ways? Has God brought family or friends into your life to help you see the harm in your destructive ways, but you have not listened? Have you been participating in your patterns of self-hate for so long you consider it a friend instead of your enemy? If any of these questions apply to you, please explain how.

Some examples of things we could "love" that are our enemies, and things we hate that actually love us or are good for us:

LOVE (have an affection for)	HATE
Abusive boyfriend	parents who really love you
Razor for cutting	friends who tell you to stop
Alcohol, cigarettes, drugs	normal life
Seeing the numbers drop on the scale	calories
Junk food eaten in secret	talking about life problems
Premarital sex	being alone

Earth things

What would you add to the list?

friends who really care about you

84

Fill in the blanks of Zechariah 10:2 (the second to last book of the Old Testament).

"The idols speak _Lies_, diviners see visions that _are false_; they tell dreams that are _Empty_, they give comfort in _vain._"

Fill in the blanks of 1 Samuel 12:21.

"Do not turn away after _following_ idols. They can do you _servent_ _given_, nor can they _Save_ you, because they are _idols_.

The things or persons we look to for comfort outside of God have fooled and misled us. Let them fool us no more as we embrace the Truth. Letting go of our false comforts will bring about a freedom in us to see our True Comforter in Christ. If you need to cry, go ahead. It is alright to grieve your loss, but know that greater joy awaits you. Crying helps relieve stress—but remember to let go and move on. A greater victory awaits you.

As you move on, think and consider something you can do positively to replace the destructive way. There will be a void in your life as you learn to live without your false comfort. Now is a great time to take up a new hobby, join a club on campus, volunteer at your church, or get a job. Now is also a great time to throw away your razor, break-up with an abusive boyfriend, not go to parties where there is drinking and/or smoking, or get professional help for an eating disorder. God says in Isaiah 57:18,19 "'I have seen his ways, but I will heal him. I will guide him and restore comfort to him, creating praise on the lips of the mourners in Israel. Peace, peace, to those far and near,' says the LORD. 'And I will heal them.'"

Let's pray:

Dear heavenly Father, I pray that I will have no other gods before me. I pray that I will trust and serve you with all of my heart. You have been so faithful to me. Guide me as I let go of my self-hate and cling only to You, my King. In Jesus' name I pray, Amen.

Day 5: Profound Mystery

Today's Scripture:

This is a profound mystery—but I am talking about Christ and the church.
Ephesians 5:32

We began this Bible study by thinking about our longings. We studied Scripture and concluded that God allows us to long so we will ultimately cry out to Him. We then prepare ourselves for the day our King comes to get us, His bride, and take us to His eternal kingdom of heaven. This is the storybook, fairytale ending is it not? To live happily ever after? Hollywood has certainly captured the innate God-given dream that each of us has to live happily ever after. But, not only do we want to live happily ever after, we want to be with the one man who is captivated by our beauty, has rescued us from danger, and delivered us from a mediocre life.

Seriously, I know you have thought about this theme of "happily ever after" and have seen it played out in movie after movie. Jot down some of your favorite movies that end with the scenario of a man and woman falling in love and then supposedly living happily ever after.

- "Zoo"
- "Raiponse" - Cendrillon et autres
- "John Carter"

This dream of finding someone, falling in love, and living happily together is given to us at birth by God so that our hearts would seek Him. Hollywood has captured this dream by idealizing the earthly relationship between a man and a woman especially in the Walt Disney Princess films that we watched as little girls. These films caused our hearts to believe that the perfect man will make all our dreams come true.

Do you see what Satan has done with our hearts? Girls, we are so vulnerable in the area of romance. Satan has been watching and studying relationships between a man and a woman since Adam and Eve. He has had thousands of years of experience and knows the female tendencies and lures our affection toward something or someone and away from our Ultimate Man, God Himself. Since we were little girls, Satan has been slowly stealing our hearts away from God's perfect, unfailing, unconditional, undying love for us. Unless we have been living in a cave somewhere, I do believe each of us have had our hearts deluded (lied to) in the area of romance. My pastor says to Christians, "It isn't that we don't need to love God more; it is that we need to understand how much He loves us."

Jesus Loves Me

Now for the fun! We get to look into one of the books of the Old Testament that is truly a profound mystery—The Song of Solomon. This book is the most intimate portrayal of our relationship with our King. I do believe it is also the literal translation describing the intimate relationship of King Solomon and his lover. (If you ever have the opportunity to study the book of The Song of Solomon, I would strongly suggest it.)

In Ephesians 5 Paul describes the godly relationship between a husband and a wife. He then says what in Ephesians 5:32 (today's verse)?

Big mystery c'est le christ et l'Eglise

With that in mind, please enjoy reading The Song of Solomon chapters 2 and 4. Write the names the Beloved (woman) is called by her Lover (man) (Example: "my darling" in verse 2).

- mon amour   - mon amie   - ma fiancée
- ma belle   - ma colombe

87

I believe these are the names God calls us in our most intimate times with Him. I believe that as we spend time alone with our King "behind closed doors," we get to know a side of Him that is not obvious otherwise. He is our Lover in the purest of ways. He is gentle and tender as He gives us His undivided attention when we pour out our burdens, dreams, fears, problems, and thoughts to Him.

Now, read the Beloved's response to her friends after they asked, "How is your beloved better than others?" in Song of Solomon 5:10-16.

Go back and read it again, but this time I want you to read it as if you were putting your head on God's chest, sitting in His lap, looking into His eyes, and taking in His sweet smell.

Describe Him—who He is personally in these intimate moments.

il Sourit et me regarde

Read Isaiah 26:3. God says He will keep us in what?

His Peace

He will keep us when our mind is what?

Trusting him

Why?

Because he loves us.

If we trust our God, really trust Him, we will want to be with Him more than anything or anyone. If we trust Him with our dreams, passions, hurts, and failures, we will want to know what He has to say. If we trust Him with our very life, we will want to be in His arms.

The King James Version of Isaiah 26:3 says, "Thou wilt keep in perfect peace whose mind is stayed on thee; because he trusteth in thee." The Hebrew word for *mind* is *yester,* which means "a form; frame, thing framed, imagination, mind." The Hebrew word for *steadfast* or *stayed* is *amah,* which means "to prop (literally or figuratively), to lean upon or take hold of, rest self, set self." Do you see God's invitation to us? When we trust Him, He has blessings of peace as we choose to prop our head (which frames our mind) upon Him. He desires to give us rest in this crazy life of ours. He welcomes us into His lap.

As we described who God is personally in our intimate moments, are those not the most peaceful moments of our lives? It is those moments that sustain us "though come what may."

This God who invites us to be intimate with Him is the One who is captivated by our beauty, rescues us from danger, and delivers us from a mediocre life. Want to see our Beloved who is like no other? Read Revelation 19:11-16 and Revelation 21:1-5.

Let's pray:

Dear heavenly Father, You are my Lover and I am Yours (Song of Solomon 2:16).

WEEK 5

AN INCREASED FAITH

DAY 1: INCREASE OUR FAITH

Today's Scripture:

The apostles said to the Lord, "Increase our faith!"

Luke 17:5

If we are to "set an example" in our faith as Paul instructed Timothy, I suppose that would mean we could be called "faithful"—someone who is full of faith. Hmmm . . . full of faith. What does that look like in real life?

If our goal is to be a woman full of faith, then knowing exactly what *faith* means is imperative. In the original Greek language, the word for *faith* comes from the word *pisteuo* which means (1) *to think to be true, to be persuaded of, to credit, place confidence in (1a) of the thing believed (1b1) used in the NT of the conviction and trust to which a man is impelled by a certain inner and higher prerogative and law of the soul.* Whenever we see the words *faith* or *believe* in the New Testament, these words are almost always translated from the Greek word *pistis*. Together the words *faith* and *believe* occur almost 500 times in the New Testament. As you can see, faith is

Before you dive into this week's subject, please take a moment and ask God to give you eyes to see, ears to hear, and a heart to receive His Word into your heart and mind.

an important topic in the Bible. God has a lot to say about it, but we do not have time today to cover all 500 instances! For the purpose of our study today, let's focus on the enlargement of our faith.

According to this definition of *faith,* do you think your present level of faith needs to be increased? If so, why?

Yes, cause i need to progress everyday I'm not perfect and there are things that I'm not sure

As we discuss faith, I want to focus on the relationship with our King in our present circumstances. Accepting the Lord Jesus at our time of salvation required much faith, but that is just the beginning.

Mark an "x" to indicate where your faith in God is at this particular time in your life.

Doubt God's activity in my life	My belief in God is strong one day, weak the next	Believe God wholeheartedly

What area(s) in your life require(s) a great deal of faith?

Future,

What do you believe to be the greatest obstacles (something or someone that gets in your way) to your faith?

bad Friends, temptations...

Let's read the context of today's scripture. Please read Luke 17:3-6. In your own words, what was Jesus teaching the disciples (and us) in verses 3, 4?

To forgive

How did the disciples respond?

They said they wanted a bigger and stronger faith

Jesus was teaching us to forgive others who have wronged us numerous times even in a single day. In the Luke passage, the person of whom Jesus spoke must have known the person being wronged because he kept coming back to ask for forgiveness.

Is there someone in your life who wrongs/hurts you every time you turn around? Maybe it's someone as close as a roommate or parent or sibling. The situation may not be changing, but as you choose to forgive, your heart and perspective toward the person and situation will be changed for your good and God's glory.

Forgiveness = Faith

I love the disciples' response to Jesus' teaching, but I also have to say that I am a bit baffled. What does faith have to do with forgiveness? What is it that we need to believe in order to forgive?

When we forgive someone, it means we have relinquished the right to hold a grudge, lay blame, get even, or seek justice. We forgive. We let go. This is scary because we are trusting that God is in control of the situation. We are admitting that we cannot control the other person or punish the other person. It's out of our hands, and we forgive. The offense is no longer charged to his or her account.

During Christ's teaching session in Luke 17, Jesus set the standard really high in regard to forgiveness. Not to mention in the previous two chapters, He had been doing some pretty hefty talking about what it really means to be a follower of God. The disciples (as do we) felt extremely overwhelmed, realizing that they couldn't accomplish this type of forgiveness on their own. They cried out, "Increase our faith." How did Christ answer? Reread Luke 17:6. Jesus gave them an indication of how small their faith really was. If they only had a small amount of faith—the size of a mustard seed (one of the smallest seeds)—then they could do miraculous things! But Jesus was saying you do not even have that! Ouch.

A great way to begin to enlarge your faith is to start with the foundational practice of forgiveness. Without much thought, you already have a list of people you know you need to forgive. More than likely that's the Holy Spirit bringing these thoughts to your mind because He knows about the resentment, bitterness, and hurt you're holding onto. Let go of that sin. Have faith that God is who He said He was. Like the disciples, we realize that we cannot live up to God's standards. We cannot be a perfect God follower. But like the disciples as well, we have the Holy Spirit to help us, teach us, and guide us into obedience. Write down the names of the people you need to forgive, then pray the prayer at the end of today's lesson.

Let's pray:

Dear heavenly Father, I do need more faith. I do believe you have my best interest in mind, so I choose to trust You in this particular area of my life. I need to forgive ___My Parents___ *. Please teach me what it means to forgive completely and guide me to live out this forgiveness. I trust You to help me in this area. Father, increase my faith! In Jesus' name I pray, Amen.*

Day 2: Completely Amazed

Today's Scripture:

They were completely amazed, for they had not understood about the loaves; their hearts were hardened.

Mark 6:51b, 52

The disciples crack me up. Throughout our study we have seen them on several occasions where they have acted like little children. Remember in Week 1, Day 1 we overheard them arguing about who was the greatest? Then, yesterday we read about Jesus' lesson on forgiveness. They responded by basically saying, "How can we do that?" Yes, at first I laugh at them, but my laughter usually ends in humility when I begin to look at my own lack of faith.

Yesterday I had you list obstacles of your faith. Please review your answers and add more if you like.

Reading stories of God's miracles and other's faith in action (or lack of!) can teach us excellent lessons. Let us look at a couple to see what we can learn. Please read a familiar, yet amazing text of Scripture found in Mark 6:30-44.

Can you hear the disciple's response to Jesus telling them to feed 5,000 plus people (verse 37)? In your own words, what did they say in response to Jesus?

That it was to expensive, and they didn't really want to feed them

Once again, we see the disciples thinking in the natural rather than the supernatural. In the natural, it was obvious they could not provide food for so many, but Jesus showed them supernatural provision.

Can you think of a time when God provided for your family supernaturally? Maybe it was in purchasing a house, car, or paying for tuition. Maybe it was in providing food or clothes or money for a bill. Briefly describe God's supernatural intervention and then tell Him of your thankfulness. (If you cannot think of an instance when God provided supernaturally for you, but you have heard of Him providing for another family, please describe the event.)

He brought a house in Sweden for us, and a beatiful one.!

Please continue reading in Mark 6:45-52. Write out verse 48:

Alors, versla fin de la nuit, jesus viens vers eux en marchant sur l'eau, il ventles depasser.

This verse makes me laugh out loud even with no one else in the room. Read it again. The disciples were struggling with the oars against the wind. Jesus had told them to get into the boat and go to the other side, and now they can barely row. At the time of their struggle, Jesus, unbeknownst to them is walking on the same turbulent waters. What makes me laugh is that Jesus "intended to pass by them (NASB)." I can just see Jesus going on His merry way to the other side. Although the disciples are struggling, He does not force His help. But as soon as the disciples cried out to Him, what three things does Jesus do (verses 50,51)?

Talk, sit in the boat, and the wind stops

Isn't this a wonderful time to see the word *immediately* in Scripture? Immediately He spoke to them, identified Himself, and got into the boat. With Him by their side, the wind stopped. According to verse 51 how did the disciples react to the wind stopping?

They were chocked

Depending on your translation of verse 51, you may have written, "they were greatly astonished," "they were completely amazed," or "they were sore amazed in themselves beyond measure, and wondered." We have to keep in mind that just a few hours before the disciples had witnessed an extraordinary miracle when Jesus fed the 5,000 with five loaves of bread and two fish. Not only that, but 12 baskets were left over. They were there, they experienced the miracle, and they fed each person food. Now these guys are beside themselves with amazement and wonder because they saw Jesus walk on the water and felt the wind stop as soon as Jesus got into the boat. It was almost as if they did not know Jesus had supernatural power. These guys were not amazed because of excitement, joy, or celebration. They were amazed because they could not believe what had just happened. They were in disbelief. The NASB states verse 52 in a great way, "for they had not gained any insight from the incident of the loaves, but their heart was hardened."

"…but their heart was hardened." A hard heart was the disciple's obstacle to faith, understanding completely who Jesus was, and what He could do. Does a hard heart hinder your faith?

yes

If they had learned from the incident with the loaves, would their reaction to the wind and seeing Jesus walk on the water have been different?

Yes

Hard Heart Attack

We, too, can be like the disciples when we take for granted what Jesus has already done for us, and then doubt Him in a present circumstance. We, too, may have a hardened heart that blocks us from having a heart full of faith to believe God.

You have listed obstacles to your faith, now explain the root of these obstacles. Dig deep and write about why these obstacles are so troubling to you.

Cause this is not what God wants and what is good this is the world things

Let's pray:

Dear heavenly Father, Thank You for all you have done for me. Thank you for all You have done for my family. Forgive me for doubting You. I pray that if I do have a hard heart, that You will expose the pieces of my hardened heart so that I can more fully believe You. Help me overcome the obstacles to my faith. You are so good to me. I praise Your holy name. In Jesus' name I pray, Amen.

Day 3: A Heart of Flesh

Today's Scripture:

I will give them an undivided heart and put a new spirit in them; I will remove from them their heart of stone and give them a heart of flesh.

Ezekiel 11:19

From yesterday's lesson, what did we identify as an obstacle to our faith?

a hard heart

Most of us probably do not think we have a hard heart. After all, we are doing this Bible study and many other godly activities. How could our hearts be hard or dull if we do all of these things? According to today's Scripture, we see that our hearts can be divided. Our hearts can be hardened in one area of our lives and softened in other areas.

What do I mean by a hard heart? A hard heart or "heart of stone" is a part of our inner being that builds a wall towards God or other people. It's a defensive mechanism built around our hearts to protect us from being truly seen by others or to keep us from being hurt. Once this wall is in place, each time we keep ourselves from getting too close to someone, that place in our heart gets harder. It's also known as a calloused heart. It's one layer at a time being built upon another. We may have subconsciously put the first layer on our heart and not even realized what we were doing; then, our reaction and responses become automatic. We automatically resist others for fear of being vulnerable and eventually wounded.

The same applies to our relationship with God. Our sinful nature disconnects us from God and we can not comprehend Him—who He is, how much He loves us, how He redeems us, etc. So when others hurt and disappoint us, we apply those human qualities to God: "I can't trust God. What if He fails me just like my mom did?" "I can't ask God for forgiveness because He probably gets angry just like my dad." "I can't tell God my secret hurts. What if He exposes me like my friend did?" Before we know it, we do not recognize when God speaks or works in our lives . . . because we will not be vulnerable. We have built the wall. After a while, we even stop caring. God, who?

Real Freedom

Why do we have hardened hearts? When did we put that beginning layer over a portion of our heart? There could be numerous answers to these questions, but I am convinced that unforgiveness has something to do with it. Can you remember a time in your childhood when you trusted someone and they let you down—they failed you by disappointing you? It could be over something very simple and childish, and yet you are still bothered by it even as you think on it now.

I told a secret to a friend and she told it to everyone

What fears, hurts, etc have you transferred from your past to your relationship with God?

I gave all my hurts fears etc to God, all of my "baggage"

Realizing and naming these areas are a BIG step. But you do not have to stop there. Freedom from this baggage is possible. God promises you a heart of "flesh."

Please read Ezekiel 11:18-21. Fill in the blanks to verse 19.

"I will give them an _**undivided**_ heart and put a _**new**_ spirit in them; I will remove from them their heart of _**stone**_ and give them a heart of _**flesh**_."

We identified earlier what a heart of stone meant, now let us identify what replaces the heart of stone. God calls this new heart a heart of what according to verse 19?

of flesh

The word *flesh* in the Hebrew is *basar*. This word comes from another Hebrew word *basar* which means *to be fresh, full, rosy, cheerful*. It also means *to announce (good news)*.

Instead of a callous, dull, or dead heart, God lavishes us with a heart that is fresh and full and has something to be cheerful about. He gives LIFE! Not only do we have good news to share about eternal salvation from hell, but we can also share with others how Jesus has set us free from fears we face on earth! It becomes easier to believe who God says we are because we do not have the obstacle of a hard heart.

Look at Ezekiel 11:20. After God gives us a heart of flesh, what are we told to do?

Respect his law and rules

Look up the words *faithful* and *faithfulness* in a Bible concordance. Then, look up all the verses you can find about God's faithfulness. Let these verses be a reminder and an encouragement to you when you are tempted to doubt God's perfection. He can't and won't fail you. You are free to trust Him with your whole heart!

Why do you think obeying God's Word is important in the context of God giving us a heart of flesh?

Because if he gives us a heart of flesh we have to be thankful and we have to obey him, because we have a relationship with him.

I am sure your answer includes the fact that God does not want our hearts to become hardened again. He is smart, isn't He? Obviously, one of God's laws is to forgive. We are to forgive those listed above for intentionally or unintentionally hurting us. Go ahead. With the Lord at your side, you can do this. Say this prayer aloud. *Dear heavenly Father, by an act of my will, I choose to forgive _____ for hurting me physically and/or emotionally. I realize he/she does not know the depths by which this has hurt me. I hold nothing against this one. I loose myself from him/her and bring myself under Your cross where I find healing and restoration. I forgive him/her as you have so mercifully forgiven me. I bless _____ and ask Your blessing upon him/her. In Jesus' name I pray, Amen.*

Awesome. Now that we have confessed and forgiven, God has the amazing opportunity to soften that once hard spot in our heart. The next time someone hurts our feelings, let us be quick to forgive to keep our hearts fresh and cheerful.

In conclusion, look at what God tells Isaiah can happen if we allow God to remove our heart of stone and give us a heart of flesh. Read Isaiah 6:10 and list the benefits to our eyes, ears, hearts and lives when we turn to God.

In the space provided, write out a prayer of thanksgiving to God for removing your hard heart and replacing it with a new, fresh heart that has some good news to share.

Let's pray:

Seigneur,
Je te prie d'enlever mon cœur de pierre qui
fait que je n'ai pas une entière relation avec toi
dans la confiance, l'amour et la foi. Je te prie de
me donner ce cœur de chair pour que je fasse entièrement en relation
avec toi et aide moi à respecter ta loi. Au nom de Jésus. Amen.

Day 4: When She Heard

Today's Scripture:

When she heard about Jesus, she came up behind him in the crowd and touched his cloak, because she thought, "If I just touch his clothes, I will be healed."
Mark 5:27, 28

Please read Mark 5:21-34 and imagine yourself being this unnamed woman. What is your favorite verse or part in this story?

Verse 34

As Jesus was on His way to heal a synagogue ruler's daughter who was dying, He was surrounded on all sides by a large crowd of people. Among the people was a woman who was deemed unclean by the Hebrew law because of her bleeding.

Old Testament Tip: According to Leviticus 15:25-33, if anyone touched the hemorrhaging woman, they would be ceremonially unclean, and would have to go through procedures to be clean again. In other words, this woman was not supposed to be there because of the strict laws placed upon her. But, verse 26 reveals the woman's desperation and the urgency of her need. We can assume that most of the woman's past 12 years had been spent pursuing healing. We don't know how old this woman was, but we can certainly, as women ourselves, feel for her as she had had a period for 12 years with no relief. In fact, she got worse instead of better. Name a time in your life you had a physical or spiritual problem that over time worsened? (A spiritual problem could be an internal struggle you have had with sin, or maybe a prayer request you have prayed for years that has not been answered with an affirmative.)

"When she heard about Jesus…" I want us to pause for a moment and let those words penetrate our hearts. "When she heard about Jesus…" I believe that this is the moment she grasped faith. Let's examine a few Scriptures just prior to this incident. Look up the Scriptures and record how she heard about Jesus and what she had heard.

Mark 1:28, 39, 45:

Whole region of Galilee, new tleach and cure. Chassaitles demons, by a ma who cried out what Jesus did

Mark 3:7,8: heard about him from lots of parts of the world

Mark 5:18-20:

Then said to everyone what Jesus did to him

Similarly, have you heard something about Jesus that has fueled your faith?

the story of 2 people that had ~~a thing~~ were sick, very dangeras we can die and they didn't die, Jesus saved them

Romans 10:17 fuels my faith. I want to show it to you from the Amplified Bible. "So faith comes by hearing [what is told], and what is heard comes by the preaching [of the message that came from the lips] of Christ (the Messiah Himself)." What is so awesome about what this woman "heard" from others is that the message really did come literally from the lips of the Messiah Himself on this earth. What we "hear" too comes directly from the mouth of Jesus when we read His Word, but I can not help but think that these people who lived during Jesus' day really did hear an audible voice! This woman (I sure wish we knew her name) had heard of the many miraculous healings Jesus had done for those in need, and obviously in desperation knew He could do the same for her. Do you believe what God has done for others, He will do for you?

Yes because he loves me like the others

She was a woman full of faith. What this woman hoped would happen when she touched His clothes came true. This is another wonderful time in Scripture we see the word *immediately*. "Immediately her bleeding stopped..." (Mark 5:29).

Have you had a prayer answered in the affirmative "immediately"? If so, how did that affect your faith in God?

Wasn't Thy mom ~~didn't~~ arriving to grab me and my sister I prayed and she arrived imediately, My faith has really grown up

Tell the Truth

Take one last look at the woman whom Jesus healed of her 12 year infirmity. After Jesus realized power had gone out from Him, He sought the one who had touched Him. The woman must have known He was looking for her because she came to Him in complete humility and fell at His feet. She told Him the whole truth.

I don't want you to miss this next truth. It isn't worth it to hide from Jesus, nor to tell Him only part of the truth. Healing of your body and/or soul is at stake. Had this woman run off, she would have missed the biggest blessing of her life. She came to Him in fear, and left His presence in peace. The word *truth* in verse 33 implies "as not concealing." Princess, you don't have to hide anymore. Fall at the feet of Jesus, tell Him everything, and then live in peace. Peace with God, peace in your circumstances, and peace with others. It may also be necessary for you to tell someone else the "whole truth." Is there someone you have only told partial truth in a particular circumstance? Please pray if God may be leading you to humble yourself and tell the truth to someone from whom you are hiding.

Let me pray for you. Receive this prayer over your life.

Dear heavenly Father, I pray on behalf of this dear sister and princess. King of kings, I ask that you will give her courage to obey You. I pray that You will reveal to her any area of her life that she may be hiding from You or from someone else. Help her to see and to know that she is safe and protected by Your love for her. Help her also to understand that the truth really does set her free. Bless her and grant her peace. In Jesus' name I pray, Amen.

He said to her, "Daughter, your faith has healed you. Go in peace and be freed from your suffering."

Mark 5:34

Day 5: Promise of God

Today's Scripture:

Yet he did not waver through unbelief regarding the promise of God, but was strengthened in his faith and gave glory to God, being fully persuaded that God had power to do what he had promised.

Romans 4:20, 21

Today we have the privilege of seeing a man in the Bible who like the hemorrhaging woman had a body that was progressively getting worse and yet, he too, believed against all human hope.

Carefully read Romans 4:18-22 and answer the following questions.

What promise was given to Abraham (verse 18)?

He will be the father of a very big nation

How could this promise seem like a hopeless cause (verse 19)?

He was old and his wife couldn't have childs

Was Abraham's faith wishy-washy (verse 20)?

Not at all! :)

In my opinion, Abraham did something profound. What did he do before he ever saw the fulfillment of the promise (verse 20)?

he was stronger in his faith and glorified God.

What did Abraham believe God had in order to do what He had promised (verse 21)?

He can do what he promised

Old Testament Tip: This account of Abraham is fully described in Genesis 17 and 18. Genesis is one of my very favorite books of the Bible. It is rich with amazing stories of God interacting with His people. On your own, you may want to go back and read of Abraham and his wife, Sarah. Abraham was 75 years old when God first told him that he would be a father of many nations (Genesis 12). The fulfillment of God's promise did not happen until 25 years later! Most of us cannot comprehend ever waiting that long to see a promise fulfilled in our lives.

Romans 4 wonderfully summarizes Abraham's testimony of faith, and pushes us to want to believe God in our own circumstances. Hebrews 11:11 gives us a little insight into Abraham's faith. According to this verse, why did Abraham not waver in his faith?

Cause Sara believed too

There are a lot of people who make promises to us—the president of the U.S., governor, teachers, parents, friends, boyfriends—and yet how much do we really trust them to keep their promises? My young daughters really do believe that when someone promises something to them, it WILL happen. They do not take into account the weather, finances, or unexpected situations. If they are promised something, they expect it. That is exactly why I never promise them anything. My oldest tries to get me to say "I promise," but I rarely do because I know something may happen to keep me from following through with the promise. I do not want to disappoint her or her sisters. Promises are a big deal!

Can you think of a promise someone made to you that they were unable to keep?

My dad promised me to go to a shop and after we havent been there

How did that make you feel?

Bad and sad

Do you have a hard time believing God's promises?

Yes, I think sometimes...

Without looking in your Bible, name as many promises of God that you can remember.

Abrahams promises, The promess of Jesus to come, the Holy spirit to come, That he will give us a hope and a future, the promess that he will come back to take us...

God gave Abraham a promise that he would be a father to many nations. God even told Abraham that his offspring would be as many as there are stars in the sky (Genesis 15:5). God specifically spoke this promise of blessing over Abraham and yet in the natural realm it seemed impossible. Romans 4:20, 21 (today's Scripture) says that in the course of the 25 years of waiting, Abraham's faith grew strong. On Day 1 of this week we looked at the Greek word for faith. Go back and reread the definition for *pisteuo*. Does Abraham's faith in God fit the definition of faith? If so, how?

Yes, cause he is persuaded of this thing promess.

God Gets the Credit

How do we get that type of faith to believe like Abraham? First and foremost, we need to know what God promises us. Obviously, we can only believe for something that we are aware of biblically. God's Word is full of promises for any need, situation, relationship, or personal problem. Second, we must not waver in our belief. If we know what God has said to us, we need to speak it as truth and not doubt that God can and will do what He says He can do. I am convicted of believing one thing, then saying just the opposite to a friend. That is not true belief. Just as Abraham gave God the glory before the fulfillment of the promise, so we need to give God the credit due Him even in our conversations with others.

I want to share with you a personal testimony of believing God because I know that I am not the only one who has struggled in this particular area.

A lot of us as little girls were afraid of the dark. We would be too afraid to go to the other side of the house to the bathroom alone; we went to sleep in fear of what was under our bed or in our closet; we were afraid to go into the dark garage; or we were fearful to close our eyes not knowing what is happening around us. What is silly about all of these fears is that during the day we have no problem doing any of them. Our fears come upon us when it is dark. I grew up being scared of the dark. As I got older it didn't get any better—my fears just transferred into different areas. I became fearful of getting into my car at night; I was afraid of being home alone; and I was fearful when I woke up in the middle of the night. The magnitude of my fears escalated after I was married when my husband had to be out of town. It was miserable for me to make myself go to bed. I did not like being afraid. I wanted to be strong. But, because of my history of being scared, it was an automatic reaction, especially when I was alone at night. Finally, I learned to believe what God said instead of being fearful. I decided to take to heart and lean on Psalm 4:8.

In the space below, write Psalm 4:8.

Je me couche et aussitôt je m'endors en paix, car c'est toi seul Eternel, qui me donne la sécurité dans ma demeure

This verse was my ticket to freedom. God said I can have peace not just as I am sleeping, but even in my lying down. You see, my biggest struggle was turning off my nightstand light and putting my head on my pillow. I memorized Psalm 4:8 and said it over and over as I was preparing for bed. I could feel the presence of God with me as I meditated on His Word and believed I was safe. He was pleased that I believed Him (Hebrew 11:6). He comforted me just as a father tucks his child into bed and says

111

everything is going to be alright. By believing the truth of God's Word, I overcame my fear of the dark.

In whatever present circumstance you find yourself, ask God to give you a specific Scripture to stand on and believe. Write the Scripture on an index card and say it back to Your heavenly Father as many times as the need arises. He is so eager to bless you, provide for you, protect you, save you, heal you, sustain you, minister to you, and to speak to you. Will you let Him?

 Yes

Let's pray:

Dear heavenly Father, You are my Savior, my Provider, my Protector, my Healer, my Shepherd, and my Rock. I thank You for being believable. I thank You for the faith You've given to me through the Holy Spirit. I pray that my faith in you will grow strong as I meditate on Your Word and believe You to do the impossible in my life. As I wait, sustain me with Your grace. I love You. In Jesus' name I pray, Amen.

WEEK 6

BEING PURE

Day 1: You Were

Today's Scripture:

But you were washed, you were sanctified, you were justified in the name of the Lord Jesus Christ and by the Spirit of our God.

1 Corinthians 6:11

Please do not skip out on this week's study because of the subject matter. I realize there are exceptional resources available on purity, and you have probably heard many messages emphasizing the need for sexual purity, especially in today's culture. You may have been to a weekend retreat focusing entirely on purity, or even taught it to younger students. Having done all of these and maybe more, I still believe God has something new to teach you and me. Yes, even me. Just because I am married does not mean I am exempt from keeping myself pure. Your adventure in purity by no means ends on your honeymoon; it just takes a different form. Even in my married life, purity is something Satan wants to rob from me. Married women still have to keep a guard against attacks from the enemy. See if you can fill in the blanks (without looking in your Bible) to our theme verse for Chapters 2-6. "Don't let anyone look down on you because you are young, but set an _example_ for the believers in _Speech_, in _Life_, in _Love_, in _faith_, and in _purity_," (1 Timothy 4:12).

God has ordained you and me to set an example to others in your purity. Paul believed Timothy was capable of setting an example in the five areas because Paul had taught and trained Timothy. God has provided us with His Word, teachers, pastors, counselors, and the Holy Spirit to teach and train us. God believes we have the capabilities through Him. Unfortunately, in the area of purity we may not have too many people to follow, but I believe you can be the one. Even if you or one of your friends have strayed from purity in the past, it is not too late to set an example. Today is another "new day" to make a choice to walk in new ways pleasing to the Lord. Do not consider yourself as "out" or "disqualified." You are still breathing and have an obvious desire to be all God wants you to be (as evidenced by participating in this study), so keep your head up and run this race of life confident in who you *are* in Christ.

Princess, in Christ you *are* pure. We are not trying to obtain purity, we *are* pure. According to 1 John 1:7, 9 who purifies us and from what?

Jesus, from sin

According to Acts 15:9 what is required of us as God purifies us?

Faith

By accepting Jesus and confessing we have sinned, by faith we believe God purifies or cleanses us. At salvation we are made pure. We believe we are clean or pure through faith. We trust that what God says He will do, He will. Then, we walk by faith which means we have the right to walk as a pure princess.

Is this concept new to you? Did you at one time think you had to work at being pure? Do you now understand that God has made you clean because of what Jesus did for us on the cross? Write your thoughts.

> Not really,
> Yes, cause it something very important
> ... I think yes

A Pure Princess

Please read 1 Corinthians 6:9-11, then write the word immediately following the word *were* in verse 11 (*were* appears four times, so list four different words).

> Loves
> Justes
> declares saints

Paul described the sins of the people, and then reminded them that God had made them different from the world; different in such a way that they no longer were to identify themselves as sinners. Paul reminded them they were washed, sanctified, and justified in the name of Jesus Christ. Today, I want to remind you of your identity in Christ. At your day of salvation your sins were washed away by Jesus' blood on the cross. You were sanctified, meaning you were declared holy and pure in God's eyes. You were justified in that you are free from the punishment of death and regarded as a saint. This is why you can walk with your head held high because you do not need to feel guilty about your sin. When you do sin, quickly come before God and ask for forgiveness. Then believe by faith that you are forgiven.

As a pure princess in Christ, our responsibility is stated simply in 1 Timothy 5:22: "Keep yourself pure." The original Greek word for pure is *hagnos* which means *clean, innocent, modest, perfect: chaste, clean, pure.* The word *chaste* in Webster's Dictionary means "morally pure in thought and conduct; decent; modest. Not having experienced sexual intercourse; virginal."

Let's make a "Do" and "Don't" list describing practical things to help us maintain our purity. I will begin the list and then you can add to it.

Do	Don't
Read the Bible daily	Read gossip magazines
Wear modest, cute clothing	Wear clothes to gain attention
Set boundaries with boyfriend	Cross over your boundaries
Be where you are supposed to	Skip classes

You will be blessed as you "keep yourself pure." Write out Matthew 5:8:

"Heureux ceux qui ont le coeur pur car ils verront Dieu"

Let's pray:

Dear heavenly Father, I am pure because You sent Jesus to die and rise again so I can be washed, sanctified, and justified. I trust You and Your Word and believe by faith that You do what You say You will do. I pray I will set an example in my purity. I need You. I love You. In Jesus' name I pray, Amen.

Day 2: Spirit, Soul, and Body

Today's Scripture:

May God Himself, the God of peace, sanctify you through and through. May your whole spirit, soul, and body be kept blameless at the coming of our Lord Jesus Christ. The one who calls you is faithful and he will do it.

1 Thessalonians 5:23-24

It is challenging in today's culture to maintain purity. It really is. Your generation is bombarded with obvious as well as subtle lures that tempt you to compromise your standards of purity. From pornography to billboards; commercials to song lyrics, the world awakens our sexuality in ways God never intended for our eyes to see, our ears to hear, our hands to touch, or our heart to feel. The pull to think, to act, and to look like the world is stronger than we realize. We can be drawn to think contrary to God and not even know it. That's why it is so important not to act primarily on your feelings, but by what you know to be the truth. To maintain purity, you have to know the Truth—Jesus.

Yesterday's study is vital truth because if we truly grasp our identity in Christ that we *are* pure, then we are less likely to act otherwise.

"Remember, he (Satan) wants to make the clean feel unclean in hopes that they will act unclean."

Beth Moore in *When Godly People Do Ungodly Things.*

Do you think the world has more to offer than God? Why or why not?

No, cause God offersus everlasting life, love, truth...

Do your actions back up your beliefs?

Sometimes...

God created humans and divided our being into three different parts – spirit, soul, and body. As believers our sexuality is a unique aspect of our character because sexuality affects our spirit, soul, and body. Our spirit is dead when we are born, then becomes alive after accepting Jesus. When we participate in sexual activity we affect our spirit either by using it for sinful purposes or in God's way through marriage. As believers, sex in marriage transcends another aspect that non-believers cannot fathom because we are given the gift of connecting with our spouse in the Lord.

Our soul consists of our mind, will, and emotions; it exemplifies our personality. When we participate in sexual activity we affect our soul by giving of an extremely intimate part of our personality. Sexual activity also affects our soul in that we experience another type of "love" (*eros* – the romantic type).

Our body is obviously our physical body. When we participate in sexual activity we directly affect our body. Sexual activity can also directly affect our body later through disease or pregnancy.

Because sexual activity affects all three parts—spirit, soul, and body—I believe this is one reason why Satan attacks us through our sexuality. He knows that sexual activity can do a lot of damage spiritually, emotionally, and physically. One thing I hoped you have learned from *Royal By Blood* is that as a princess in Christ you have an enemy. This enemy, Satan, does not want God to be glorified, honored, or reverenced so he tempts Christians to sin in ways that undermine God's powerful work in us. Attacking our sexuality is perfect because sexual sins carry long term effects.

According to 1 Thessalonians 5:23, 24 (today's Scripture) who sanctifies us through and through?

God the father

Who is to keep our spirit, soul, and body blameless?

Us

Does God give up on us? How is God described in verse 24?

No, he is described like that; "I vois a appelen it eot fidele,"

Blameless means to be faultless or without blame. Some of you have been robbed of your innocence as children from a predator. In those times, you are *not* to be blamed. It was *not* your fault. Jesus cares so much for you, and He cares about what happened. Read the seriousness God takes in matters of someone wronging a child in Luke

119

17:1,2.

God will avenge the predator; you can be sure of it. For you, precious one, in order for your complete healing, you need to take a step of faith (if you have not already done so) and choose to forgive your predator. Also, if you have not shared your story with an older, wise woman of God, now is the time to seek comfort and counsel through someone who loves you. My prayer for you is Proverbs 31:25 "Strength and dignity are her clothing. And she smiles at the future" (NASB).

God's Temple

Read 1 Corinthians 6:18-20. How does verse 18 describe sexual sin as different from other sins?

It's a sin of our own selves that affects us.

What does it mean to you that your body is the temple of God?

God is in us, he is holy and pure, and so the temple need to be clean, pure.

Paul is not stating that sexual sin is more of a sin than others, but that it is different because when a man has sex with a woman, he enters her body. The word *against* in the original Greek language means "into" or "entering a place." Even though you can sin by putting drugs into your body, Paul differentiates sexual sin from any other sin. As we discussed in Week 4 Day 5, the sexual union between a man and woman is what the Bible uses to illustrate the intimate relationship God has with His children (Song of Solomon and Ephesians 5:32). Committing sexual sin with our body mocks God's love for us and mocks the marriage union He ordained.

Fill in the blanks to 2 Corinthians 7:1.

"Since we have these promises dear friends, let us ___*purifie*___ ourselves

from ___*sin*___ that contaminates ___*the body*___ and

___*Spirit*___ perfecting holiness out of ___*Cramie*___ for God."

Our whole being—spirit, soul, and body—is created to bring glory, honor, and reverence to our King. The Holy Spirit indwelling us is one of the greatest mysteries of the New Testament (Colossians 1:27). It is also one of the greatest privileges of believers this side of the cross. As you know, with great privilege comes great responsibility. First Corinthians 6:18 instructs us to "flee sexual immorality," which means to run from the dangers of impurity in thought, word, and deed. Let's run from danger and to the one who calls us beautiful. "The king is enthralled by your beauty; honor him, for he is your lord," (Psalm 45:11).

Let's pray:

Dear heavenly Father, I want to honor you with my spirit, soul and body. Convict me of any ways I am dishonoring You. Forgive me for _____. Help me to honor You in ways I have never thought of before. I am beautiful to You, my King. You are my Lord. I honor You. In Jesus' name I pray, Amen.

Day 3: Noble Purposes

Today's Scripture:

If a man cleanses himself from the latter, he will be an instrument for noble purposes, made holy, useful to the Master and prepared to do any good work.

2 Timothy 2:21

One thing we learned from 1 Corinthians 6:19 is that our body is the temple of the Holy Spirit. In the Old Testament the Israelites had to go to a literal place, the temple or tabernacle, to be in the presence of God. The tabernacle consisted of three parts: outer court, Holy Place, and Most Holy Place. The outer court is where the Israelites gave their animals to be sacrificed to the priests. The only ones allowed into the Holy Place were the priests who were responsible for the articles in it. The only one allowed in the Most Holy Place, which was separated from the Holy Place with a veil, was the High Priest who could only enter once a year and under strict regulations. In the Most Holy Place was the ark of the covenant where God's presence would manifest. It was in the tabernacle that the believers brought their animals to be sacrificed as a sin offering that freed them from the guilt of their sins.

Read through Leviticus 8:1-15, 30. In verse 11, what did Moses do with some of the oil?

> times on the autel, ustensiles,...

What was the purpose of the anointing oil?

To consacrate, to make these things pure.

In verse 30 what did Moses do with some of the oil and some of the blood? What was the purpose?

He put some on Aaron and his sons and their chothes

To consecrate it, make it pure.

24/7 Access

Fifty chapters in the Bible are devoted to the Old Testament tabernacle. The specific instructions and details given to the structure and the priests were significant to God and should be to us too. When Jesus was born on the earth, the tabernacle took on a new form in the body of Jesus. John 1:14 says, "The Word became flesh and made his dwelling among us." "Dwelling" means "tabernacled." Jesus became the tabernacle in His flesh. What was God pleased to do according to Colossians 1:19, 20?

To reconciler the world and the heaven through the blood of Jesus christ.

When Jesus died on the cross what happened to the veil (curtain) in the temple (Luke 23:45)?

It has been broken

The torn veil symbolizes that believers now have direct access to God's presence. After the resurrection and before His ascension to heaven, Jesus told the disciples that when He leaves God will send the Holy Spirit to indwell them (Acts 1:8). Second Corinthians 1:21, 22 tells us that God "anointed us, set his seal of ownership on us, and put his Spirit in our hearts."

Please read the marvelous words of Hebrews 10:19-22. Not only have we been anointed, but we have been sprinkled spiritually with Jesus' blood so that we can be cleansed or consecrated (made holy). Does knowing your body is the temple of God mean more to you now? Explain how.

Yes, cause he lives in us ...

Having this insight, fill in the blanks to 1 Corinthians 6:15: "Do you not know that your

_____*body*_____ are _____*a part*_____ of Christ himself?"

The *International Bible Commentary* describes 1 Corinthians 6:15: "His possession of us is physical as well as spiritual. Hence the horror of using parts of His body for fornication." Fornication is when someone sins in the area of sexual activity.

Now, I want to put what we studied about the Old Testament tabernacle together with the new tabernacle of our body. (You're doing so well; don't stop now!)

Please read the short account in Daniel 5:1-4. What did King Belshazzar order brought to him at the great banquet?

The golds and silvers glass.
wp

From where had these items originated?

From the temple of God.

The items were part of the articles that had been anointed, sprinkled, and consecrated to use in the sacred ceremonies in the temple. The king made a huge mistake by using holy vessels in an unholy way. His actions mocked (made fun of) the glory, honor, and reverence of God. Princess, the private parts of our bodies are sacred and only to be touched or seen by our husband after we say our vows. Just as this king abused the sacredness of the gold goblets by using them for partying pleasures, Satan wants us to use our sacred body parts for pleasures outside of God's will.

Look in Daniel 5:30 and write what happened to King Belshazzar that very night of the banquet.

He has been killed

God does take seriously the treasures He anoints, sprinkles, and consecrates. It grieves God when we choose to present our body as if it were unholy. It grieves Him because He has good things planned for us, but when we choose to disobey, He can not bless. He has done so much for you and me through the cross. And yet, He is not finished giving to us. But God can take what was once used for unholy purposes and use them again for holy purposes. The goblets the king used were even used again after the temple was rebuilt in Jerusalem (Ezra 8:28, 29).

Today's verse in the *Amplified Bible* says, "So whoever cleanses himself (from what is ignoble *and* unclean, who separates himself from contact with contaminating and corrupting influences) will [then himself] be a vessel set apart *and* useful for honorable and noble purposes, consecrated *and* profitable to the Master, fit and ready for any good work." Maintaining our purity is not limited to avoiding sexual intercourse. Maintaining our purity is exemplified in how we wear our clothes. Do

"Teenagers worry that they will miss out on something if they heed the Bible's warning against premarital sex. Actually, the warnings are there to *keep* them from missing out on something. Fidelity sets a boundary in which sex can run free."

- Philip Yancey,
Rumors of Another World

our shirts completely cover our breasts? Are our skirts and shorts too short? Purity is maintained as you set boundaries with your boyfriend in where he touches you. Purity is maintained as we confess our sin and turn from it even if it means breaking up with a boyfriend or not hanging out with particular ungodly influences. Purity is maintained in how we speak about our sacred body. Purity is maintained as we wait for our future husband who will have godly access to our most sacred parts in a way that truly brings glory, honor, and reverence to our King.

Let's pray:

Dear heavenly Father, It is amazing to know that You have made my body with such detail and sacredness even as You did with the tabernacle. I want to be ready for any good work you have for me.

I want to be ready for the day You come and get me, Your bride. In Jesus' name I pray, Amen.

Day 4: She Led Him

Today's Scripture:

With persuasive words she led him astray; she seduced him with her smooth talk.
Proverbs 7:21

Today, let us examine ourselves through the mirror of the Proverbs 7 woman. Today's study will give us insight into some deep places of our soul. David prayed in Psalm 51:6, "Surely you desire truth in the inner parts; you teach me wisdom in the inmost place." Proverbs 7 is about a woman who discovered her "power" and used it wrongly.

"When we discovered as young women that our curvaceous bodies or pretty faces would turn heads, it awakened us to a form of power that was intoxicating…perhaps even addicting. Turning the head of a peer became a small thrill, while turning the head of an older, important man held huge payoffs for our egos. Whether it was the captain of the football team, the college professor, or the head of the department at work, sharing in the power of important people by aligning ourselves with them in relationship gave us a distorted sense of significance."

Shannon Ethridge, *Every Woman's Battle*

By no means is today's study making any accusations. My intention for us to study Proverbs 7 is to alert us to some possible thoughts or actions we have or may have in the future so we can be prevented from continuing or putting ourselves in a sinful behavior pattern. The Lord has used this proverb in my life at different seasons to warn and convict me. I don't believe this proverb is just about a non-believer; any one of us could slowly be in her position if we do not take deliberate preventive actions. We need to be wise in our influence with a man. We need to be wise in our vulnerabilities. Proverbs 7 is written about a married woman, but it has much to teach single women. Before we go to Proverbs 7, Read 2 Corinthians 11:3. According to this verse, can a person who genuinely serves God be deceived?

No yes

Just like Eve was deceived, so can we. When we are deceived, we soon deceive others. Please read all of Proverbs 7 s-l-o-w-l-y.

To whom is the Proverb written (verse 1)?

A son

According to verses 2 and 4 what does the father say his son needs?

He has to keep the wisdom, a keep the "lessons" of his father as the apple of his eyes

Can you hear how emphatic the father is with his son? The father is strongly advising his son to cling to his commands, teachings, wisdom, and understanding. The father knows that the most vulnerable to seduction (to be led astray) is the one who lacks judgment (verse 7).

What time of day did the seduction take place (verse 9)?

The end of the day, when the night is "arriving"

What is different about the night that would attract this type of trouble that maybe would not be as likely in the daylight?

At night nobody sees ya... so at night we are busy.

One thing for sure that is different in the night is the way loneliness sets in. During the day we are busy going to classes, running errands, or working where we are around people whether they are friends or strangers. When evening comes, we want to be with someone to talk about the day or just hang out. We want to be with someone who really knows us and likes us. I believe one reason we do things in the night that we would not during the day is to avoid feeling lonely. Verse 11 tells us that she is never at home. We are not told why she does not want to be at home, but we do know that she is being rebellious against something or someone. Have you ever been like that? Have you ever wanted to be anywhere but home? If so, why?

Sometimes, because I was angry, My parents got me angry, tomy brothers and sisters too...

How was the Proverbs 7 woman dressed (verse 10)?

Like a prostitute

Worth the Cost?

She was not a prostitute, but resembled one. She knew that by dressing as she did, she could be noticed by a man. We know too, don't we? We know the shirts and the dresses that give us the most looks. What I have found to be true is that the guys who desire godliness in their own lives will choose a girl who demonstrates godliness in her clothing. Guys are territorial by nature. They do not want us to be revealing in our outfits because they do not want anyone else to see our body, and they really do want to wait until the honeymoon to "unveil" us. Men also love mysteries, adventure, and romance. Too much too soon—they go on to someone else.

Look again at verses 13-18. The woman seduced the young man through all five of his senses. Write the verse that applies to each of the senses. (Fellowship offerings mean she was able to bring home some of the meat from the animal sacrificed.)

Touch

kiss, v.13

Taste

_14_

Hearing

_16 – 17_

Sight

_10_

Smell

_17_

This woman knows what she is doing. She understands a man's needs and within

129

a few minutes she has captivated him perversely. The scariest and saddest part of this Scripture is verse 14. She actually went to "church" that same day. She said she fulfilled her vows, which means she made "peace" offerings between herself and God. Let's not be one person with our friends at church and another person outside of church. We will have peace with ourselves and God when we are consistent with our talk and our walk.

Verse 21 says that she led him astray with her seductive words. We can not always blame the guy. Sometimes our appearance and the things we say and do can lead us (and someone else) down a wrong path. In verse 22 what is his following her compared to?

like a beef & that is going to be killed

What will this "fun" cost him (verse 23)?

hurts his heart, he doesn't know that his life is in danger

Do you think it was worth the cost?

Yes

The Proverbs 7 woman was needy, empty, and dissatisfied. She had a husband but thought she needed more. Her wrong actions not only affected her, but also many others. Your dating life will have an affect on you and many others for years to come. Intimate relationships have a profound impact on all involved. Your presence is a gift to someone; choose whom you want to give it to.

Turn in your Bible to Proverbs 4:23. Fill in the blanks. "Above all else, ___*be careful what you think*___ your ___*mind*___, for it is the ___*depositing*___ of life."

As a princess in Christ you are to protect your heart from lies by knowing who you are and obeying what you know to be true. Your life flows from what is within your heart. Be an example to those around you by showing that God has purified your heart and that you believe you are pure. There is no need to seek guys to validate you. You have all you need in Jesus!

Let's pray:

Dear heavenly Father, You have given me all I need in Your son, Jesus. I pray You will fill me up with Your Holy Spirit. I pray that I will use my influence with men in godly ways. In Jesus' name I pray, Amen

Day 5: Made Clean

Today's Scripture:

The voice spoke to him a second time, "Do not call anything impure that God has made clean."
Acts 10:15

As we begin our last day, I wonder if you are feeling the same way I am? I did not know if I would ever make it to the end. Has this Bible study taken you longer than 6 weeks to complete? Maybe it has been a whole semester or even a year. No matter, we are here together . . . on the last day. I have thoroughly enjoyed every day. My prayer for you is that you and your King have had many memorable moments together as you opened His Word. I hope you experienced His gentleness and tenderness toward you and your circumstances. I pray you will continue to hunger and thirst for His presence in your life.

A few years ago our family went to Glorieta, New Mexico for Collegiate Week at the LifeWay Conference Center, which is located in the Rocky Mountains. While my husband and I went to our classes, the girls went to Kid's Camp. Because of being in the mountains, the girls always got dirty at camp and loved it! After several days of getting in late from camp and classes and the girls still needing baths when it was already past their bedtimes, I came up with a new plan for the last two days. After dinner and before their last camp session, I decided to give them their baths. Then, when we got in from the evening activities all they would have to do was change into their pajamas, brush their teeth, and go to bed. But, that meant the girls could not play in the dirt at the evening camp session. So, I reminded them many times before I dropped them off that they were clean. It did not mean they could not play or have fun, it meant they could not sit down in the dirt and play with rocks and sticks. The morning and afternoon camp sessions were their opportunities to play in the dirt.

As I would remind the girls that they had already had their baths and that they were clean, the Lord spoke to my heart. He wanted me to know that the times He has cleansed me by forgiving me of my sins, that He forgives not out of duty, but because He really does love me. When He forgives me I am made clean again. Just as I told my girls, "Remember you are clean," He too wants me to remember I am clean so that I do not continue sinning. I can not make myself clean; it is something only He can do for me. If my girls had "forgotten" they were clean and had played in the dirt, I would have given them another bath and forgiven them. He even more will tenderly wash you as you come to Him.   Psalm 19:12, 13 is a great prayer; write it out in the space below.

God doesn't want to take away our fun just as I did not want to with my girls. There were still many other fun activities they could do at camp like swinging, playing inside games, and singing around the campfire. God's abundant life for us is experienced in the context of His plans which give us a hope and a future as we obey Him. He calls us to obey Him specifically in our sexuality so we can experience His most satisfying and guiltless sex life in marriage with one partner. Life in Christ is not boring.

If you have some "dirt" on you now, do not be scared to talk to your heavenly Father. (You know, you can't hide from Him). God has the bath water already drawn and soap and a towel ready. He will forgive you when you ask Him. Do not hesitate, call His name and allow Him to cleanse you. He knows your sin and still loves you. "While we were still sinners Christ died for us" (Romans 5:8). Even before we were ever made clean, Christ did the ultimate to make us clean by becoming sin and canceling our debt and nailing it to the cross. That, Princess, is the good news of Jesus Christ.
Do not worry about what other people may say. You know what God has done for you. You know what He says about you. They may remember what the "old" you did, but that is not the "new" you. When you remember the "old" you, tell yourself that that part of you has died. You, Princess, are royal by *His* blood.

To end, write out and memorize these verses. These are the basic truths God wants you to carry through your life. If these are engrained in your heart and mind, Satan will have lost a large part of his battle against your life!

Psalm 139:7:

Jeremiah 19:11:

Voici ce que déclare le Seigneur de l'univers : je casserai ce peuple et cette ville comme on casse une cruche d'argile, ce sera irrémédiable.

Romans 5:8:

Mais Dieu nous a prouvé à quel point il nous aime, Christ est mort pour nous alors que nous étions encore pécheurs.

Galatians 2:20:

De sorte que ce n'est plus moi qui vit à mais c'est le Christ qui vit en moi car ma vie humaine je la vit dans la foi au fils de Dieu qui m'a aimé et donné sa vie pour moi.

Colossians 2:13, 14:

Spirituellement mort pour nos fautes mais Dieu vous a fait revivre par le Christ, il a annulé le document qui nous accusait.

Let's pray:

Dear heavenly Father, I die to myself today and choose to live for You. You are my King, my God, my everything. In Jesus' name I pray, Amen.

Visit **www.randallhouse.com** and receive a free Leader's Guide for *Royal By Blood.* Discover tools to aid you in leading your small group through a six-week study exploring the role of royalty as well as the role of a servant the believer is called to fulfill in God's family. In this on-line resource you will find practical insights for group discussion and suggested extras for each week. You will also find a personal note from Jennifer Johnson.

To order additional copies of
Royal By Blood

call **1-800-877-7030** or
log onto **www.randallhouse.com.**

Call for quantity discounts.

Experience

the Power Behind the Passages
You've Known for Years

Verses We Know By Heart
Jennifer Devlin

$10.99- Group Discounts Available!
ISBN: 9780892655656

Verses We Know By Heart is a six-week study of familiar Old Testament passages. Throughout this study, you will gain a more insightful look into the background, context, and meaning of each passage. The variety of topics applies to various stages of life and will ignite you with a passion to search the Word of God for truths needed to overcome all of life's obstacles.

The Verses We Know By Heart study covers these following passages:
- *Genesis 1:1—2:3*
- *Exodus 20:1-17*
- *Proverbs 3:5-6*
- *Psalm 23*
- *Ecclesiastes 3:1-14*
- *Isaiah 40:10-31*

randall house

**To order call 1-800-877-7030
or visit www.randallhouse.com**

Printed in the United States
104264LV00003B/1-202/A

9 780892 655700